TO:

_____

FROM:

_____

DATE:

_____

BIBLE PROMISES
— FOR THE —
ENNEAGRAM

LIVE YOUR FAITH

Bible Promises for the Enneagram
Copyright © DaySpring Cards, Inc. All rights reserved.
First Edition, January 2021

Published by:

21154 Highway 16 E
Siloam Springs, AR 72761
dayspring.com

Produced with the assistance of Peachtree Publishing Services
Cover Design by Lauren Purtle

Printed in China
Prime: J3111

ISBN: 978-1-64454-848-6

– **Contents** –

Introduction...7

TYPE 1

Overview...9
Strengths...10
Key Challenges...12
Needs...14
Ones in the Bible..16
Key Scriptures...18
A Prayer for Ones...27

TYPE 2

Overview...29
Strengths...30
Key Challenges...32
Needs...34
Twos in the Bible..36
Key Scriptures...38
A Prayer for Twos...47

TYPE 3

Overview...49
Strengths...50
Key Challenges...52
Needs...54
Threes in the Bible...56
Key Scriptures...58
A Prayer for Threes..67

TYPE 4

Overview...69
Strengths...70
Key Challenges...72
Needs...74
Fours in the Bible...76
Key Scriptures...78
A Prayer for Fours..87

TYPE 5

Overview...89
Strengths...90
Key Challenges...92
Needs...94
Fives in the Bible..96
Key Scriptures...98
A Prayer for Fives...107

– Contents –

TYPE 6

Overview..109
Strengths...110
Key Challenges.......................................112
Needs...114
Sixes in the Bible....................................116
Key Scriptures..118
A Prayer for Sixes..................................127

TYPE 7

Overview..129
Strengths...130
Key Challenges.......................................132
Needs...134
Sevens in the Bible................................136
Key Scriptures..138
A Prayer for Sevens...............................147

TYPE 8

Overview..149
Strengths...150
Key Challenges.......................................152
Needs...154
Eights in the Bible..................................156
Key Scriptures..158
A Prayer for Eights................................167

TYPE 9

Overview..169
Strengths...170
Key Challenges.......................................172
Needs...174
Nines in the Bible...................................176
Key Scriptures..178
A Prayer for Nines.................................187

At-a-Glance Reference Guide...............188

– Introduction –

This book uses the popular Enneagram as a framework to help point people to the promises that are found in God's Word. While the Enneagram types are not based on any specific biblical teaching, learning about our personal gifts, attributes, weaknesses, and strengths can help us apply biblical principles to our lives in meaningful ways. As we engage with the Enneagram, we can better understand how God created us to think, act, and respond within our relationships with Him and with the people around us.

Just as the different characteristics of the Enneagram types can be seen in our own personalities, these characteristics are also evident in biblical characters—people who faced many of the same struggles we do and were in need of God in the same ways we are. We have selected one character of the Bible for each of the nine Enneagram types as a way to highlight the attributes common to each type. We can learn about ourselves from the actions and decisions made by the people we read about in the Bible.

The Enneagram is a helpful tool that people—even Christians—can engage with to help us discover more about our character and what drives us. This book organizes the strengths, challenges, and needs of people based on their Enneagram types and then provides a number of Bible verses that can offer comfort and encouragement for people struggling with different challenges and needs. Our hope is that this little book will help you discover more of the promises God has in store for you in His Word.

– Type –

THE REFORMER

The Rational, Idealistic Type
PRINCIPLED
PURPOSEFUL
SELF-CONTROLLED
PERFECTIONISTIC

– Overview –

Ones are model citizens. They are conscientious, trustworthy, self-controlled, and responsible. They are also ambitious, driven by an inner critic that constantly compels them to be—and make things—good.

Ones all-too-clearly see imperfections in the world, in themselves, and in others. They also have a deep desire to do something about those imperfections. So Ones work hard to improve, to succeed, to bring order from chaos.

Ones struggle with perfectionism. They see need for reform and improvement everywhere, so their work is never done.

At their best, Ones can size up a situation and quickly determine the right course of action. They have a deep understanding of humanity and are able to see hope and potential in the midst of the flaws. They inspire others with their integrity.

In a work setting, Ones maintain high standards and will work hard to meet them. However, they may clash with coworkers who aren't as committed as they are.

– Strengths –

- Ones are self-motivated. They don't need any-one to coax or inspire them to act. Ones see what needs to be done and then do it.

- Ones are honest. They can be counted on to of-fer a fair assessment. They can be trusted to tell the truth, even when the truth is hard to hear.

- Ones are ethical. They are motivated to do the right thing instead of the thing that will benefit them most.

- Ones are detail oriented. They sweat the small stuff that often gets overlooked in the big picture.

– Strengths –

- Ones are agents of change. When they throw their considerable capacity for hard work behind a social cause, they can impact the lives of many people.

- Ones are conscientious. They take their obligations seriously. They can be counted on to follow through on what they say they will do.

- Ones are practical. They know how to find workable solutions to problems. They resist the urge to indulge in magical thinking.

- Ones value improvement. They work hard to make the world a better place and to make themselves better people.

– Key Challenges –

- Ones must overcome the misconceptions of others who may see them as judgmental, critical, and closed-minded. In order to do that, Ones must be willing to show the "cracks" in their perfect facade and make themselves vulnerable.

- Ones must recognize that often "perfect is the enemy of good." In striving for perfection, instead of being satisfied with "good enough," Ones can end up undermining the progress they strive for.

- Ones must acknowledge that being good or being right will not earn the love and approval they seek from other people.

- Ones must learn to embrace imperfections and flaws as being part of every person's unique character. Likewise, they must learn to embrace mistakes as learning opportunities.

– Key Challenges –

- Ones must always look for opportunities and reasons to feel love for others. Love keeps feelings of resentment and judgment at bay.

- Ones must separate themselves from the inner voice telling them that things aren't good enough—or that they aren't good enough.

- Ones must embrace serenity—the stilling of their perfectionistic hearts. They must learn to incorporate compassion and patience into their worldview.

- Ones must learn to change what can be changed, accept what can't be changed, and learn to recognize the difference between the two.

– Needs –

- Ones need routine and structure. They work best when they know the rules and understand the expectations that others have for them.

- Ones need to protect themselves from deep disappointment. The pain of discovering that the world is far from perfect motivates them to try to construct a perfect personal universe.

- Ones need to maintain their self-image of being right and upstanding. The pressure to keep up appearances is something that drives Ones to work so hard.

- Ones need justice. They need affirmation that good prevails in the end, that evil is punished, and that hard work is rewarded.

– Needs –

- Ones need worthy causes. They need to fight for things that are worthwhile. They need to be involved in projects that result in dramatic transformation or improvement.

- Ones need to maintain self-control, especially when it comes to their emotions. They feel as though they have to keep a lid on their feelings, passions, and desires, at the risk of hurting themselves or others.

- Ones need to satisfy their powerful inner critic that judges their thoughts, words, and deeds. Compliments from others mean little to Ones if their inner critic isn't satisfied.

Ones in the Bible
PAUL

The common link between Saul, the zealous Jew who tried his best to destroy Christianity, and Paul, the missionary who advanced the cause of Christ more than anyone besides Jesus Himself, is the idealistic Reformer we see in both guises. In his pre- and post-conversion iterations, the man from Tarsus was a textbook example of a One.

As Saul, he was driven by his passion for Jewish law. He built his reputation on his scrupulous adherence to the rules and regulations of Judaism. His zeal for his Jewish faith was so extreme that he was prepared to murder those he believed were defiling it. He was consumed with being the perfect Jew.

As Paul, he was driven to reform the world in the name Jesus, whom he had once persecuted. His zeal for the Lord surpassed even his zeal for Judaism. He immersed himself in the teachings of Christ and then carefully reconfigured his entire life in order to live according to them.

Only a highly functioning One could say, in all humility, as Paul does in I Corinthians 11:1, "You should imitate me, just as I imitate Christ" (NLT). He could say that because he carefully managed his actions and interactions. Case in point: he refused to accept the financial support that was due him as an apostle because he didn't want to be a burden to anyone. Paul imitated Christ to the best of his ability so that others could imitate his Christlikeness.

Paul drew on his experience as a One to combat the Jewish false teachers who infiltrated first-century Christian congregations. These teachers tried to draw on their own authority and credentials to intimidate the new Christians. Paul countered their credentials with his own, which were nearly perfect by those teachers' standards. He was an alpha One, and though it embarrassed him to have to do it, he was perfectly willing to draw on his carefully cultivated reputation in order to protect his spiritual children.

– Key Scriptures –

WHEN YOU NEED ENCOURAGEMENT

Not that I have already obtained this or am already perfect, but I press on to make it my own, because Christ Jesus has made me his own. Brothers, I do not consider that I have made it my own. But one thing I do: forgetting what lies behind and straining forward to what lies ahead, I press on toward the goal for the prize of the upward call of God in Christ Jesus.

PHILIPPIANS 3:12–14 ESV

WHEN YOU FEEL RESPONSIBLE FOR MAKING THINGS RIGHT

Do your own work well, and then you will have something to be proud of. But don't compare yourself with others. We each must carry our own load.

GALATIANS 6:4–5 CEV

– Key Scriptures –

WHEN YOU FEEL RESENTFUL

Get rid of all bitterness, rage and anger, brawling
and slander, along with every form of malice. Be
kind and compassionate to one another, forgiving
each other, just as in Christ God forgave you.

EPHESIANS 4:31–32 NIV

WHEN YOU FEEL UNWORTHY

How great is our Lord! His power is absolute! His
understanding is beyond comprehension!
The LORD supports the humble, but He brings
the wicked down into the dust.

PSALM 147:5-6 NLT

– Key Scriptures –

WHEN YOU CAN'T FORGIVE YOURSELF

He does not deal with us according to our sins, nor
repay us according to our iniquities. For as high
as the heavens are above the earth, so great is his
steadfast love toward those who fear him.

PSALM 103:10–11 ESV

WHEN YOU SHUT DOWN YOUR FEELINGS

Praise God, the Father of our Lord Jesus Christ!
The Father is a merciful God, who always gives us
comfort. He comforts us when we are in trouble, so
that we can share that same comfort with others in
trouble. We share in the terrible sufferings of Christ,
but also in the wonderful comfort He gives.

II CORINTHIANS 1:3–5 CEV

– Key Scriptures –

WHEN YOU NEED WISDOM

My son, if you accept my words and store up my commands within you, listening closely to wisdom and directing your heart to understanding; furthermore, if you call out to insight and lift your voice to understanding, if you seek it like silver and search for it like hidden treasure, then you will understand the fear of the LORD and discover the knowledge of God.

PROVERBS 2:1-5 CSB

WHEN YOU NEED APPROVAL

I am not trying to please people. I want to please God. Do you think I am trying to please people? If I were doing that, I would not be a servant of Christ.

GALATIANS 1:10 CEV

– Key Scriptures –

WHEN YOU COMPARE YOURSELF TO OTHERS

Oh, don't worry; we wouldn't dare say that we are as wonderful as these other men who tell you how important they are! But they are only comparing themselves with each other, using themselves as the standard of measurement. How ignorant!

II CORINTHIANS 10:12 NLT

WHEN PEOPLE QUESTION YOUR INTEGRITY

Blessed are you when they revile and persecute you, and say all kinds of evil against you falsely for My sake. Rejoice and be exceedingly glad, for great is your reward in heaven, for so they persecuted the prophets who were before you.

MATTHEW 5:11-12 NKJV

– Key Scriptures –

WHEN YOUR INNER CRITIC WON'T BE QUIET

Do not let any unwholesome talk come out of your mouths, but only what is helpful for building others up according to their needs, that it may benefit those who listen.

EPHESIANS 4:29 NIV

WHEN YOU NEED INSPIRATION

So whoever knows the right thing to do and fails to do it, for him it is sin.

JAMES 4:17 ESV

WHEN YOU SEE AN OPPORTUNITY FOR REAL CHANGE

I have told you these things so that in Me you may have peace. You will have suffering in this world. Be courageous! I have conquered the world.

JOHN 16:33 CSB

– Key Scriptures –

WHEN YOU STRUGGLE WITH PERFECTIONISM

But he said to me, "My grace is sufficient for you, for my power is made perfect in weakness." Therefore I will boast all the more gladly of my weaknesses, so that the power of Christ may rest upon me. For the sake of Christ, then, I am content with weaknesses, insults, hardships, persecutions, and calamities. For when I am weak, then I am strong.

II CORINTHIANS 12:9–10 ESV

WHEN YOU GET ANGRY

He who is slow to wrath has great understanding, but he who is impulsive exalts folly.

PROVERBS 14:29 NKJV

– Key Scriptures –

WHEN YOU'RE TEMPTED TO CRITICIZE OTHERS

So in everything, do to others what you would have them do to you, for this sums up the Law and the Prophets.

MATTHEW 7:12 NIV

WHEN YOU FEEL MISUNDERSTOOD

We can say with confidence and a clear conscience that we have lived with a God-given holiness and sincerity in all our dealings. We have depended on God's grace, not on our own human wisdom. That is how we have conducted ourselves before the world, and especially toward you. Our letters have been straightforward, and there is nothing written between the lines and nothing you can't understand. I hope someday you will fully understand us, even if you don't understand us now.

II CORINTHIANS 1:12–14 NLT

– Key Scriptures –

WHEN YOU NEED MOTIVATION

And let us not grow weary while doing good, for in due season we shall reap if we do not lose heart. Therefore, as we have opportunity, let us do good to all, especially to those who are of the household of faith.

GALATIANS 6:9–10 NKJV

WHEN YOU DON'T LIKE
HOW YOU FEEL ABOUT YOURSELF

For we are his workmanship, created in Christ Jesus for good works, which God prepared beforehand, that we should walk in them.

EPHESIANS 2:10 ESV

WHEN YOU MUST ACCEPT
WHAT CAN'T BE CHANGED

Even a courageous person's steps are determined by the LORD, so how can anyone understand his own way?

PROVERBS 20:24 CSB

A Prayer for
ONES

Gracious heavenly Father, I praise You and humbly thank You for the sacrifice of Your Son. His blood has cleansed me of my imperfections. I am now wholly acceptable to You. Let me never lose sight of that truth.

Help me extend to others the grace that You've shown me. Remove the judgmental attitudes from my spirit.

Let Your Holy Spirit nurture forgiveness in my heart so that I may forgive others—and myself—for not living up to my expectations. Break down the barriers within me that keep me from fully expressing my love, and help me understand how much You truly love me.

Guide my actions and efforts to improve the world around me. Help me imitate Christ in the way I live and in the choices I make, so that others can imitate me.

In Jesus' name. Amen.

– Type –

THE HELPER

2

The Caring, Interpersonal Type

GENEROUS

DEMONSTRATIVE

PEOPLE-PLEASING

POSSESSIVE

– Overview –

Twos connect with other people by working to make life better for them. You can recognize Twos by their empathy, sincerity, generosity, and willingness to sacrifice their own needs for the sake of others. They set a high bar for themselves as friends, family members, and coworkers—and then strive to clear it. They find joy in helping others. They take pride in their helping skills.

Twos help people see positive qualities in themselves. They offer companionship and a listening ear. They have an instinct for recognizing people's needs and finding ways to meet them.

At their best, Twos live life with a servant's heart. They model the kind of unselfishness and altruism that others aspire to.

In a work setting, Twos are conscientious and emotionally intelligent. Their heightened skills in reading other people, their desire to please, and their strong work ethic will make any organization better.

– Strengths –

- Twos are loving. They forge relationships that are strong and deep. They are willing to sacrifice for the sake of others.

- Twos are compassionate. They feel genuine concern for others. Twos are moved to act when they see people who are hurting or struggling.

- Twos are adaptable. They find ways to be helpful, regardless of circumstances.

- Twos are nurturing. They see potential in other people and find ways to bring it out.

- Twos are generous. They eagerly share their resources, time, attention, and energy.

– Strengths –

- Twos are supportive. They are quick to offer words of encouragement and motivation. They are staunch defenders when others try to discourage or question people's plans. Twos say and do the things that are necessary to help people succeed.

- Twos are tuned in to other people's feelings. They can sense when something is wrong. They are not fooled by people who try to hide their emotions.

- Twos are empathetic listeners. In conversation, they encourage people to open up. They ask questions that draw people out. They give people a safe place to share their needs and concerns.

– Key Challenges –

- Twos see themselves as important when other people see them as important. If they don't get the acceptance and affirmation they desire from others, they will be tempted to change something about themselves in order to get it. In worst-case scenarios, they open themselves up to manipulation and rejection.

- Twos need to make sure they are ministering to themselves so they can effectively minister to others. As Jesus demonstrated during His earthly ministry, that involves regular time alone with God. Twos who make a priority of being energized and fed by Him will be able to operate from a position of strength.

– Key Challenges –

- Twos need boundaries. They need to know when their efforts to help become intrusive. Workable boundaries help Twos maintain a sense of identity and value apart from their relationships with others.

- Twos must find a way to belong—to a family, a group of friends, a church, or some other community. They need to feel a sense of connection with other people. Within their groups, Twos need to feel appreciation for who they are.

- Twos must walk a fine line between self-inflation and self-judgment in order to maintain a healthy self-image.

– Needs –

- Twos need to be needed. They thrive when they see themselves as being integral to someone else's well-being. They need to be aware of the good they do—and they need others to be aware of it, too.

- Twos need to express their feelings for others, in word and deed. They also need others to express their feelings for them in return. Genuine appreciation and gratitude energize Twos. When other people affirm their value as Helpers, Twos find security in their identity and purpose.

- Twos need a safe environment to vent their frustrations and dissatisfaction.

– Needs –

- Twos need to see themselves in the most positive light. In order to do that, they perform extraordinary acts of service. They go above and beyond so that others will see them as people who go above and beyond. They work hard to win love and acceptance from others.

- Twos need a sense of connectedness with other people. They work hard to establish common bonds. One of their preferred strategies is to become a go-to person for help. The way they see it, to be needed is to be connected.

- Twos need reminders to focus on themselves so that their own needs get met.

Twos in the Bible
MARTHA

LUKE 10:38–42

Jesus and His disciples arrived in a village, where a woman named Martha opened her home to them. For a Two like Martha, this was both a challenge and an opportunity. Hospitality was an essential part of the social culture of first-century Israel. People were judged by how well they were able to entertain visitors. Martha likely felt the weight of expectations when she invited Jesus into her home.

For a born Helper like Martha, this was also an opportunity to shine. She saw a chance to be needed by Jesus, and she wasn't about to let it go to waste.

Soon Martha "was distracted by all the preparations that had to be made" (verse 40 NIV). It's not hard to imagine this Two running herself ragged trying to help Jesus and His disciples by making them as comfortable as possible, preparing a memorable meal, cleaning up after them, and keeping their cups filled.

She quickly became overwhelmed—not just by her tasks but also by the inaction of her sister, Mary. While Martha attended to preparations, Mary sat at Jesus' feet and listened to Him speak. Even worse for Martha, Mary seemed to command more of Jesus' attention than Martha did. No one seemed to notice the effort she was putting in. No one seemed to need her help at that moment.

Wisely, Martha took her concerns straight to Jesus: "Lord, don't You care that my sister has left me to do the work by myself? Tell her to help me!" (verse 40). Her words are a cry on behalf of all Twos: Lord, do You care about Helpers?

Jesus showed just how much He cares by gently explaining that it wasn't the time for Martha to worry about feeding others; it was time for her to feed herself. She had an opportunity to feed her soul, and He didn't want her to get distracted by lesser needs.

– Key Scriptures –

WHEN YOU NEED ENCOURAGEMENT

Trust in the LORD and do good. Then you will live safely in the land and prosper. Take delight in the LORD, and He will give you your heart's desire.

PSALM 37:3-4 NLT

WHEN PEOPLE PULL AWAY

The righteous cry out, and the LORD hears,
and rescues them from all their troubles.
The LORD is near the brokenhearted;
He saves those crushed in spirit.

PSALM 34:17-18 CSB

– Key Scriptures –

WHEN YOU ARE TEMPTED TO CHANGE
WHO YOU ARE TO GAIN ACCEPTANCE

Your beauty should not come from outward adornment, such as elaborate hairstyles and the wearing of gold jewelry or fine clothes. Rather, it should be that of your inner self, the unfading beauty of a gentle and quiet spirit, which is of great worth in God's sight.

I PETER 3:3–4 NIV

WHEN YOU HAVE DOUBTS
ABOUT YOUR VALUE

See what great love the Father has lavished on us, that we should be called children of God! And that is what we are!

I JOHN 3:1 NIV

– Key Scriptures –

WHEN YOU FEEL UNWANTED

The LORD your God wins victory after victory and is always with you. He celebrates and sings because of you, and He will refresh your life with His love.

ZEPHANIAH 3:17 CEV

WHEN YOU FEEL UNAPPRECIATED

In fact, some parts of the body that seem weakest and least important are actually the most necessary. And the parts we regard as less honorable are those we clothe with the greatest care. So we carefully protect those parts that should not be seen.

I CORINTHIANS 12:22–23 NLT

– Key Scriptures –

WHEN YOU NEED A VERBAL HUG

Come to Me, all you who are weary and burdened, and I will give you rest. Take My yoke upon you and learn from Me, for I am gentle and humble in heart, and you will find rest for your souls. For My yoke is easy and My burden is light.

MATTHEW 11:28–30 NIV

WHEN YOUR STRUGGLES BECOME OVERWHELMING

Therefore don't worry about tomorrow, because tomorrow will worry about itself. Each day has enough trouble of its own.

MATTHEW 6:34 CSB

– Key Scriptures –

WHEN YOU KNOW SOMETHING NEEDS TO CHANGE

Search me, O God, and know my heart; test me and know my anxious thoughts. Point out anything in me that offends You, and lead me along the path of everlasting life.

PSALM 139:23-24 NLT

WHEN YOU HESITATE TO SHOW YOUR REAL SELF

For at one time you were darkness, but now you are light in the Lord. Walk as children of light (for the fruit of light is found in all that is good and right and true), and try to discern what is pleasing to the Lord.

EPHESIANS 5:8-10 ESV

– Key Scriptures –

WHEN YOU RECOGNIZE PASSIVE-AGGRESSIVE BEHAVIOR IN YOURSELF

Therefore be imitators of God as dear children. And walk in love, as Christ also has loved us and given Himself for us, an offering and a sacrifice to God for a sweet-smelling aroma.

EPHESIANS 5:1–2 NKJV

WHEN YOU WONDER WHETHER YOU'RE REALLY MAKING A DIFFERENCE

The King will reply, "Truly I tell you, whatever you did for one of the least of these brothers and sisters of Mine, you did for Me."

MATTHEW 25:40 NIV

– Key Scriptures –

WHEN NO ONE SEEMS TO NOTICE WHAT YOU DO

A generous person will prosper;

whoever refreshes others will be refreshed.

PROVERBS 11:25 NIV

WHEN YOU FEEL MANIPULATED

Behold, I am sending you out as sheep in the

midst of wolves, so be wise as serpents and

innocent as doves.

MATTHEW 10:16 ESV

WHEN YOU DOUBT YOUR SPECIALNESS

I chose you before I formed you in the womb;

I set you apart before you were born. I appointed

you a prophet to the nations.

JEREMIAH 1:5 CSB

– Key Scriptures –

WHEN YOU FEEL DISCONNECTED

Yes, I am the vine; you are the branches. Those who remain in Me, and I in them, will produce much fruit. For apart from Me you can do nothing.

JOHN 15:5 NLT

WHEN YOUR PRIDE IS HURT

Too much pride brings disgrace;
humility leads to honor.

PROVERBS 29:23 CEV

WHEN YOU NEED TO RECHARGE

Very early in the morning, while it was still dark, Jesus got up, left the house and went off to a solitary place, where He prayed.

MARK 1:35 NIV

– Key Scriptures –

WHEN YOU NEED INSPIRATION

So be strong and courageous! Do not be afraid and do not panic before them. For the LORD your God will personally go ahead of you. He will neither fail you nor abandon you.

DEUTERONOMY 31:6 NLT

WHEN YOU HAVE COMPLAINTS

Brothers and sisters, do not complain about one another, so that you will not be judged. Look, the judge stands at the door!

JAMES 5:9 CSB

WHEN YOU FACE CRITICISM

Whoever heeds life-giving correction will be at home among the wise. Those who disregard discipline despise themselves, but the one who heeds correction gains understanding. Wisdom's instruction is to fear the LORD, and humility comes before honor.

PROVERBS 15:31–33 NIV

A Prayer for
TWOS

You, God, stand beside me in good times and bad. You encourage me when I'm low. You give me confidence when I'm in doubt. You give me direction when I'm lost. You have shown me what it means to be a Helper, and I praise You for that.

You created within me a heart for other people. You have given me the opportunity to make a difference in people's lives. Let me never lose sight of what a profound privilege and responsibility that is.

Give me the wisdom to recognize people's needs for what they are, not for what I want them to be. Give me the discernment to know what I can and cannot offer them. Give me the endurance to be fully present when I'm needed.

Guide my actions, attitude, and motivation so that they bring honor to You.

In Jesus' name. Amen.

– Type –

THE ACHIEVER

The Success-Oriented, Pragmatic Type

ADAPTABLE

EXCELLING

DRIVEN

IMAGE-CONSCIOUS

– Overview –

Threes get things done. They find ways to be successful in even the most challenging circumstances. They have to; their self-image is based on being seen as successful. They pursue success because they need to be admired.

Threes are uniquely equipped for the modern-day business culture, where they thrive on the positive feedback they receive for their productivity. They know how to present themselves, how to network, and how to rise through the ranks.

At their best, Threes are role models. They succeed because they work hard and work smart. They also are able to acknowledge the role failure plays in building their character.

In a work setting, Threes are self-managers. They seize the initiative by taking on high-profile projects and can be counted on to complete them. They can sense other people's expectations and will work hard to fulfill those that lead them to success.

– Strengths –

- Threes are optimistic. They see the glass as half-full—and then some. Their optimism often inspires others to see the potential for success instead of failure.

- Threes are confident. They are well aware of the skills and attributes they possess. They are also well aware of their past successes.

- Threes are industrious. It's been said that Threes do more in a day than most people do in a week. Their work ethic earns them respect.

- Threes are self-motivated. They see jobs that need to be done and do them. The prospect of success-fully completing a task—and then being recognized as a success—is all the motivation they need.

– Strengths –

- Threes are energetic. They have a vitality that draws people to them. Their approach to life involves a certain degree of excitement and electricity.

- Threes are practical. Their optimism is usually grounded in reality. They have a clear sense of what is needed in order to succeed. Many create comprehensive to-do lists for guidance.

- Threes are inspiring. They have a way of making other people feel special and important.

- Threes know how to recover quickly from setbacks. They are wired to seek the next opportunity for success, so they don't stay down long.

– Key Challenges –

- Threes react strongly to other people's inefficiency and incompetence. In order to maintain healthy relationships, Threes must learn to channel their strong reactions into constructive, loving feedback.

- Threes must guard against narcissistic tendencies. In their quest to be the best, Threes walk a fine line between maximizing their potential and falling prey to vanity.

- Threes struggle to hold on to their success. They learn quickly that success is fleeting. Every day brings new demands for Threes to prove themselves again. Every day brings new opportunities to fail.

- Threes must understand that extreme competitiveness can poison a group dynamic. People find it irritating when someone constantly tries to one-up others.

– Key Challenges –

- Threes constantly compare themselves with other people. Any feelings of contentment or satisfaction can be ruined when they encounter someone they perceive as being better situated or more accomplished.

- Threes must resist the temptation to be deceptive. More than most people, Threes are inclined to embellish their résumés or exaggerate their accomplishments in order to enhance other people's opinions of them.

- The need for Threes to be "on" all the time becomes exhausting. Projecting a confident, accomplished, and successful demeanor takes a lot of work, especially when Threes don't feel confident, accomplished, or successful.

– Needs –

- Threes need to be seen as successful. They will go to great lengths to avoid failure. Seeing others who are successful ignites their competitive urges and causes them to strive harder for their own success.

- Threes need to be valued for who they are and not for what they have accomplished. They need people in their lives who can see past the trappings of success and embrace the person inside.

- Threes need to self-promote. They have an innate sense of how to present their strengths and attributes in the best possible light. If others won't broadcast their accomplishments for them, Threes will do it themselves.

– Needs –

- Threes need honest, nonjudgmental feedback. They can accept constructive criticism, as long as it's not personal.

- Threes need to create a peaceful environment. They will go out of their way to be among people who enjoy their company. They thrive when there is harmony in their surroundings.

- Threes need to provide well for their families. The well-being of their household is central to their self-image.

- Threes need space to work. Many prefer to be left alone when they are doing their jobs.

Threes in the Bible
MOSES

It should come as no surprise that God would assign one the most enormous tasks in all the Old Testament to someone who fits the classic Three profile. In the book of Exodus, the Lord recruited Moses to lead His people out of slavery in Egypt and into the Promised Land.

Though Moses was born a Hebrew slave, he was raised by Pharaoh's daughter. As a member of Egyptian royalty, he was no stranger to success and the renown it produced.

Moses reclaimed his Hebrew roots when he killed an Egyptian overseer who was beating a Hebrew slave and fled into the wilderness. We get a glimpse of his Three-centric concerns in his encounter with God at the burning bush (see EXODUS 3). Moses balked at God's command to confront Pharaoh and demand the release of the Hebrew slaves. Moses lacked confidence in his speaking ability, and he saw an opportunity not just for failure but for failure on a giant stage, which would have been a worst-case scenario for a Three like Moses.

God allowed Moses to experience success in his showdown with Pharaoh, who eventually agreed to release the Hebrews. With that boost of confidence, Moses led the people out of Egypt and into the wilderness. He rose to the challenge in classic Three fashion.

When Moses eventually failed, it struck at the heart of his insecurities as a Three. In the wilderness, God instructed Moses to bring water from a rock by speaking to it. Moses, in a moment of frustration with the always-complaining Hebrew people, struck the rock instead.

The consequence was swift and severe. God forbade Moses from entering the Promised Land. Moses failed in front of the entire Hebrew nation.

Yet that wasn't the end of Moses' story. He continued to lead the people, all the way to the Promised Land. He recovered from failure and proved his worth.

– Key Scriptures –

WHEN YOU NEED ENCOURAGEMENT

The LORD is my strength and my song; He has become my salvation. This is my God, and I will praise Him, my father's God, and I will exalt Him.

EXODUS 15:2 CSB

WHEN YOU WORK TOO MUCH

Do not wear yourself out to get rich; do not trust your own cleverness.

PROVERBS 23:4 NIV

WHEN YOU NEED TO HEAR THE TRUTH

Charm is deceptive, and beauty does not last; but a woman who fears the LORD will be greatly praised.

PROVERBS 31:30 NLT

– Key Scriptures –

WHEN YOU FEEL WORTHLESS

You surely know that your body is a temple where the Holy Spirit lives. The Spirit is in you and is a gift from God. You are no longer your own. God paid a great price for you. So use your body to honor God.

I CORINTHIANS 6:19–20 CEV

WHEN YOU'RE AFRAID

And whatever you do, do it heartily, as to the Lord and not to men, knowing that from the Lord you will receive the reward of the inheritance; for you serve the Lord Christ.

COLOSSIANS 3:23–24 NKJV

– Key Scriptures –

WHEN YOU WANT TO FEEL VALUABLE

And if you call on him as Father who judges impartially according to each one's deeds, conduct yourselves with fear throughout the time of your exile, knowing that you were ransomed from the futile ways inherited from your forefathers, not with perishable things such as silver or gold, but with the precious blood of Christ, like that of a lamb without blemish or spot.

I PETER 1:17–19 ESV

WHEN YOU HAVE TO DEAL WITH OTHER PEOPLE'S INCOMPETENCE

Love is kind and patient, never jealous, boastful, proud, or rude.

I CORINTHIANS 13:4–5 CEV

– Key Scriptures –

WHEN YOU NEED PERSPECTIVE

For our present troubles are small and won't last very long. Yet they produce for us a glory that vastly outweighs them and will last forever! So we don't look at the troubles we can see now; rather, we fix our gaze on things that cannot be seen. For the things we see now will soon be gone, but the things we cannot see will last forever.

II CORINTHIANS 4:17–18 NLT

WHEN YOU'RE A ROLE MODEL

Let your light so shine before men, that they may see your good works and glorify your Father in heaven.

MATTHEW 5:16 NKJV

– Key Scriptures –

WHEN YOU STRUGGLE WITH BEING AUTHENTIC

Love must be sincere. Hate what is evil; cling to what is good. Be devoted to one another in love. Honor one another above yourselves. Never be lacking in zeal, but keep your spiritual fervor, serving the Lord.

ROMANS 12:9–11 NIV

WHEN YOU'RE EXHAUSTED FROM BEING "ON" ALL THE TIME

Little children, let us not love in word or speech, but in action and in truth.

I JOHN 3:18 CSB

WHEN YOU FEEL THE WEIGHT OF EXPECTATIONS

No, O people, the LORD has told you what is good, and this is what He requires of you: to do what is right, to love mercy, and to walk humbly with your God.

MICAH 6:8 NLT

– Key Scriptures –

WHEN YOU DON'T KNOW WHAT YOU REALLY WANT

And Elijah came near to all the people and said, "How long will you go limping between two different opinions? If the LORD is God, follow him; but if Baal, then follow him." And the people did not answer him a word.

I KINGS 18:21 ESV

WHEN YOU FEEL APATHETIC

I know everything you have done, and you are not cold or hot. I wish you were either one or the other. But since you are lukewarm and neither cold nor hot, I will spit you out of my mouth.

REVELATION 3:15–16 CEV

– Key Scriptures –

WHEN YOU'RE CONCERNED ABOUT YOUR IMAGE

For bodily exercise profits a little, but godliness is profitable for all things, having promise of the life that now is and of that which is to come.

I TIMOTHY 4:8 NKJV

WHEN YOU NEED TO MOTIVATE OTHERS

I know what it is to be in need, and I know what it is to have plenty. I have learned the secret of being content in any and every situation, whether well fed or hungry, whether living in plenty or in want. I can do all this through Him who gives me strength.

PHILIPPIANS 4:12–13 NIV

– Key Scriptures –

WHEN YOU GET TOO COMPETITIVE

God has chosen what is insignificant and despised in the world—what is viewed as nothing—to bring to nothing what is viewed as something, so that no one may boast in His presence. It is from Him that you are in Christ Jesus, who became wisdom from God for us—our righteousness, sanctification, and redemption—in order that, as it is written: Let the one who boasts, boast in the Lord.

I CORINTHIANS 1:28–31 CSB

WHEN YOU STRUGGLE WITH PERFECTIONISM

If we say we have no sin, we deceive ourselves, and the truth is not in us.

I JOHN 1:8 ESV

– Key Scriptures –

WHEN YOU NEED TO BE MORE LOVING

Most important of all, you must sincerely love each other, because love wipes away many sins.

I PETER 4:8 CEV

**WHEN YOUR VANITY GETS
THE BETTER OF YOU**

Turn my eyes from worthless things,
and give me life through Your word.

PSALM 119:37 NLT

WHEN YOU STRUGGLE WITH JEALOUSY

But if you have bitter envy and self-seeking in your hearts, do not boast and lie against the truth. This wisdom does not descend from above, but is earthly, sensual, demonic. For where envy and self-seeking exist, confusion and every evil thing are there.

JAMES 3:14–16 NKJV

A Prayer for
THREES

O Lord, I humble myself before You. You can see beyond the surface of my identity. You see the uncertainty and neediness behind the success. You see the failures that preceded the accomplishments.

Thank You for creating within me such a powerful drive to succeed. I ask You to give me also the wisdom to know when my striving for success gets in the way of Your plans for me.

Give me the courage to embrace failure, to learn from my mistakes, and to build a self-image based on truth and not appearances.

Remind me of my worth to You. Let me never lose sight of the fact that my value comes not from impressing other people but from serving You.

In Jesus' name. Amen.

– Type –

4

THE INDIVIDUALIST

The Sensitive, Introspective Type

EXPRESSIVE

DRAMATIC

SELF-ABSORBED

TEMPERAMENTAL

– Overview –

Fours are motivated by the desire to be seen as unique and significant—anything but ordinary. Fours are sensitive and artistically gifted. They can express their feelings through music, literature, art, or performance. They use their gifts to help others recognize beauty in the world around them.

Fours often go to great lengths to demonstrate that they march to the beat of a different drum. They embrace eccentricity. They find their identity in being able to stand apart from the crowd, even as they wrestle with the desire to be accepted.

At their best, Fours are emotionally honest and eager to form bonds with other people. They provide empathy and support in their relationships. They bring passion, wit, and playfulness to the things they do.

In a work setting, Fours place a high priority on individualism. They bring a creative flair to the group dynamic but need alone time in order to thrive.

– Strengths –

- Fours are creative. They can express themselves in interesting and unique ways. They can find and create beauty.

- Fours are sensitive. They feel deeply the pains of being misunderstood or unappreciated. In turn, they will go to great lengths to prevent others from experiencing such feelings.

- Fours are introspective. They know themselves well because they spend a lot of time analyzing their emotions, decisions, reactions, and tendencies.

- Fours are emotionally honest. They recognize and acknowledge the good and the bad within themselves.

- Fours will allow others to sit in their feelings. They offer quiet support during funerals and other times of intense grief.

– Strengths –

- Fours are empathetic. They clearly see the flaws and shortcomings in themselves. As a result, Fours feel a deep connection with others who struggle with personal flaws and shortcomings.

- Fours are self-aware. They know how others perceive them because they work hard to shape other people's perceptions of them.

- Fours make life interesting. They know how to transform everyday experiences into something memorable and meaningful.

- Fours are cultured. They have a genuine appreciation for art and self-expression.

- Fours inspire others. Their willingness to embrace their eccentricities, quirkiness, and personal style can give others the courage to do the same.

– Key Challenges –

- Fours must find meaningful outlets for their creativity. They must find ways to satisfy their own need for expression while still providing meaning and enlightenment for others.

- Fours march to their own beat. Their determination to forge their path in life makes it difficult to create their desired connections with other people.

- Fours must be careful not to show disdain for "ordinary" ways of living. They must recognize and address the feelings of superiority that come from seeing themselves as unique.

- Fours must prevent their self-consciousness from getting in the way of achieving their goals.

– Key Challenges –

- Fours must recognize how their moodiness impacts their relationships. The lack of pleasure they experience in their lives may be misconstrued as a lack of interest in others.

- Fours must guard against allowing their natural melancholy to spiral into depression. They need to be aware of their emotional health.

- Fours must resist the urge to overreact when they feel misunderstood or underappreciated. Rather than withdrawing into their own internal emotional landscape, they must work hard to engage with others in order to foster understanding and appreciation.

– Needs –

- Fours need to express their uniqueness, often through their clothes, hairstyle, or other aspects of their appearance. They need others to see them as different.

- Fours need to find grounding in their inner calm. They need to look within for practical solutions to their difficulties.

- Fours need to find beauty in the world around them. They need to be able to see the sacred in ordinary things.

- Fours need to feel significant. They need to create an identity for themselves that is noteworthy in other people's eyes.

- Fours need to create meaning for themselves and others. That's why many Fours are drawn to art and creative expression.

– Needs –

- Fours need to be authentic. They are comfortable with people seeing them "warts and all," as long as they consider it an accurate representation of who they are.

- Fours need to take care of their emotional needs before they attend to anything else. Focusing on their unique appearance, at the expense of their inner selves, will leave them feeling empty.

- Fours need to counteract the feelings of shame that lurk just below the surface. They need to recognize themselves as worthy of love and attention, apart from the way they present themselves.

- Fours feel the need to attract a "rescuer." They fantasize about finding someone who will recognize the beauty of their "secret self" and save them from their unhappiness.

Fours in the Bible
SAUL

Saul, the first king of Israel, possessed the one quality that all Fours strive for: uniqueness. Saul stood out in a crowd because of his height. He was almost a foot taller than most other people (I SAMUEL 9:2).

Yet in Saul's uniqueness, we see the conflicting impulses of the Four. He looked like a king, but he didn't feel like a king. He was wracked by self-doubt, so much so that when the time came for him to be anointed, he hid (I SAMUEL 10:21–24).

As king, Saul enjoyed the privileges of power. Yet, in classic Four fashion, he struggled with envy. His envy was triggered by a seemingly minor incident early in his reign. David, a young shepherd in Saul's kingdom, had just defeated Israel's most fearsome enemy, the giant Philistine warrior Goliath. As Saul and his soldiers marched victoriously home from battle, the women of Israel celebrated them with a song: "Saul has slain his thousands, and David his tens of thousands" (I SAMUEL 18:7 NIV).

The idea of David receiving more glory than he did gnawed at the king. His envy caused Saul to go to some dark places, psychologically speaking. He allowed it to curdle into a murderous obsession. He turned his attention away from his royal responsibilities and began a single-minded pursuit to rid himself of David.

Saul allowed his unhealthy Four insecurities to fester. He turned a blind eye to everything that was good in his life and focused on what he perceived to be bad.

Saul's life spiraled out of control. His Four-ish impulse to think "outside the box" led to his dabbling in the dark arts. He consulted a medium in a last-ditch effort to save his monarchy. The medium conjured up the ghost of the prophet Samuel, who revealed that Saul would die the next day. Instead of embracing all that is good in Fours, Saul allowed his insecurities to destroy him.

– Key Scriptures –

WHEN YOU NEED TO TAKE OWNERSHIP OF YOUR CHOICES

Many are the plans in a person's heart, but it is the LORD's purpose that prevails.

PROVERBS 19:21 NIV

WHEN YOU FEEL VULNERABLE

Do not fret because of evildoers, nor be envious of the workers of iniquity. For they shall soon be cut down like the grass, and wither as the green herb. Trust in the LORD, and do good; dwell in the land, and feed on His faithfulness.

PSALM 37:1-3 NKJV

WHEN YOU STRUGGLE WITH ENVY

It's healthy to be content, but envy can eat you up.

PROVERBS 14:30 CEV

– Key Scriptures –

**WHEN YOU'RE TRYING TO PROCESS
A PAINFUL EXPERIENCE**

Therefore let those who suffer according to God's
will entrust their souls to a faithful Creator while
doing good.

I PETER 4:19 ESV

WHEN YOU ARE INSPIRING OTHERS

Make yourself an example of good works with integrity and dignity in your teaching. Your message
is to be sound beyond reproach, so that any op-
ponent will be ashamed, because he doesn't have
anything bad to say about us.

TITUS 2:7-8 CSB

– Key Scriptures –

WHEN YOU STRUGGLE WITH FEELINGS OF SHAME

I prayed to the LORD, and He answered me.
He freed me from all my fears. Those who look to
Him for help will be radiant with joy; no shadow
of shame will darken their faces.

PSALM 34:4–5 NLT

WHEN LIFE'S DRAMA GETS TO BE TOO MUCH

Make it your ambition to lead a quiet life: You
should mind your own business and work with your
hands, just as we told you, so that your daily life
may win the respect of outsiders and so that you
will not be dependent on anybody.

1 THESSALONIANS 4:11–12 NIV

– Key Scriptures –

WHEN YOUR TEMPER GETS THE BEST OF YOU

Fools vent their anger, but the wise
quietly hold it back.

PROVERBS 29:11 NLT

WHEN YOU FEEL OUT OF STEP WITH OTHERS

To everything there is a season, a time for every
purpose under heaven: a time to be born, and a
time to die; a time to plant, and a time to pluck
what is planted; a time to kill, and a time to heal; a
time to break down, and a time to build up; a time
to weep, and a time to laugh; a time to mourn, and
a time to dance; a time to cast away stones, and a
time to gather stones; a time to embrace,
and a time to refrain from embracing.

ECCLESIASTES 3:1–5 NKJV

– Key Scriptures –

WHEN YOU STRUGGLE WITH SELF-PITY

Rejoice always, pray without ceasing, give thanks in all circumstances; for this is the will of God in Christ Jesus for you. Do not quench the Spirit.

I THESSALONIANS 5:16–19 ESV

WHEN YOU DOUBT YOUR UNIQUENESS

I will praise You because I have been remarkably and wondrously made. Your works are wondrous, and I know this very well.

PSALM 139:14 CSB

WHEN YOU LOSE SIGHT OF GOD'S ROLE IN YOUR LIFE

Now this is what the LORD says—the One who created you, Jacob, and the One who formed you, Israel—"Do not fear, for I have redeemed you; I have called you by your name; you are Mine."

ISAIAH 43:1 CSB

– Key Scriptures –

WHEN YOU NEED HOPE

And the God of all grace, who called you to His eternal glory in Christ, after you have suffered a little while, will Himself restore you and make you strong, firm and steadfast. To Him be the power for ever and ever. Amen.

I PETER 5:10-11 NIV

WHEN YOU GET TOO WRAPPED UP IN YOURSELF

Do nothing out of selfish ambition or vain conceit. Rather, in humility value others above yourselves, not looking to your own interests but each of you to the interests of the others.

PHILIPPIANS 2:3-4 NIV

– Key Scriptures –

WHEN A RELATIONSHIP IS STRAINED

What is causing the quarrels and fights among you?
Don't they come from the evil desires at war within
you? You want what you don't have, so you scheme
and kill to get it. You are jealous of what others have,
but you can't get it, so you fight and wage war to
take it away from them. Yet you don't have what you
want because you don't ask God for it.

JAMES 4:1-2 NLT

WHEN YOU NEED TO KNOW
THAT GOD SEES YOU

The LORD is near to all who call upon Him, to all
who call upon Him in truth.

PSALM 145:18 NKJV

– Key Scriptures –

WHEN YOU CAN'T FIND JOY

May the God of hope fill you with all joy and peace in believing, so that by the power of the Holy Spirit you may abound in hope.

ROMANS 15:13 ESV

WHEN SOMEONE NEEDS ENCOURAGEMENT

Therefore encourage one another and build each other up as you are already doing.

I THESSALONIANS 5:11 CSB

– Key Scriptures –

WHEN YOU NEED TO SEE THE BEAUTY IN THE WORLD

Everything was created by Him, everything in heaven and on earth, everything seen and unseen, including all forces and powers, and all rulers and authorities. All things were created by God's Son, and everything was made for Him. God's Son was before all else, and by Him everything is held together.

COLOSSIANS 1:16–17 CEV

WHEN YOU FEEL LESS THAN VALUABLE

Are not five sparrows sold for two pennies? Yet not one of them is forgotten by God. Indeed, the very hairs of your head are all numbered. Don't be afraid; you are worth more than many sparrows.

LUKE 12:6-7 NIV

WHEN YOU'RE SEARCHING FOR MEANING

And we know that God causes everything to work together for the good of those who love God and are called according to His purpose for them.

ROMANS 8:28 NLT

A Prayer for
FOURS

O Lord, You have knit me together in a unique way, and I praise You for that. Let me never forget that You see me for who I am, that You love me for who I am, and that You find value in me as I am.

Thank You for the opportunities I have to express what's inside me. Give me the wisdom to recognize my feelings of shame for the destructive lies they are. Help me build an identity that is based on Your truth.

Give me a sense of appreciation for the beauty that surrounds me and for the beauty that is within me. Help me recognize that there are no ordinary things in this world because everything comes from You.

In Jesus' name. Amen.

– Type –

THE INVESTIGATOR

The Intense, Cerebral Type

PERCEPTIVE

INNOVATIVE

SECRETIVE

ISOLATED

– Overview –

Fives are driven by the need to understand the world. They focus their time and attention on examining, studying, drawing conclusions, and mastering subjects. Their self-image is built on their hard-won expertise.

Fives are driven by the desire to be seen as competent and having the necessary answers. However, the time they spend in their own heads can cause Fives to become detached from other people.

At their best, Fives can change the world. They are scholars, experts, and technicians whose breakthroughs transform the world around them and make life better for everyone. Fives cure disease, advance technology, and solve global problems.

In a work setting, Fives display flashes of brilliance. They approach challenges slowly and thoughtfully. Their tendency is to work in isolation to give themselves ample time and space for contemplation. They often need to be reminded of the importance of connecting with and reaching out to others.

– Strengths –

- Fives are curious. They will not accept things at face value. They need to dig deeper, to discover the whys and hows.

- Fives are trailblazers. They forge their own paths to knowledge and understanding. They ignore conventional wisdom until they can test it on their own terms.

- Fives are helpful. Their drive to gather knowledge and understanding is motivated by the desire to be useful to other people.

- Fives are self-reliant. They operate under the assumption that they have everything they need inside their brains. They rarely turn to others for help or support.

– Strengths –

- Fives are innovative. Their restless quest for knowledge and understanding often leads to advancements in technology and other fields.

- Fives are content to be alone. They understand the value of privacy and solitude. They will carve out the time and space they need to develop the expertise they desire.

- Fives are observant. They pay close attention to their environment and the people in it. They notice details that other people miss.

- Fives are focused. Even when they're wrestling with complex problems, Fives have the ability to block out distractions and concentrate on the task at hand.

– Key Challenges –

- Fives must understand that secrecy builds walls between people. A certain degree of openness and transparency is essential to our emotional and social well-being.

- Fives must recognize the difference between observing life and living it. They need to pursue both the satisfaction of understanding things and the thrill of experiencing them.

- Fives must find outlets for their emotions and feelings. They must integrate their inner selves and their outer selves.

- Fives must recognize the negative effects of isolation. God created us for fellowship. Though Fives may thrive intellectually by spending long stretches of time alone, they may sacrifice their social health.

– Key Challenges –

- Fives must practice generosity, even when it doesn't come naturally. Stinginess is one of the byproducts of the Five mentality, but it can be overcome with a concerted effort to share.

- Fives must remember that God intends us to share our knowledge for the benefit of everyone, instead of hoarding it for our own satisfaction.

- Fives must overcome their aversion to small talk in order to nurture a variety of relationships. Not everyone desires to converse at a high level.

- Fives must recognize the insecurity that lies at the heart of their quest for knowledge and understanding. Their fear of not being able to do things as well as others is what drives them to develop their own areas of expertise.

– Needs –

- Fives need to be useful. They thrive on being the go-to people when needs arise, as long as they feel they have something helpful and instructive to offer.

- Fives need to avoid feelings of emptiness. Their preference for isolation can cut them off from their emotions and leave them feeling very little at all.

- Fives need time to make important decisions. They are at their best when they're able to weigh their options carefully.

- Fives need to be aware of the relational sacrifices that come with their preferred method of engaging with the world. They need to recognize that the time they spend in their heads is time they're not spending with the people who care for them.

– Needs –

- Fives need independence. Many of them have a maverick streak. Their train of thought usually veers wide of conventional wisdom.

- Fives need to be seen as competent. They will go to great lengths to prepare themselves for certain situations. When those situations arise, Fives are able to validate themselves through their preparedness and competence.

- Fives need reminders to let others know that they care. When Fives share their feelings, they are often surprised by the expressions of affection they receive in return.

Fives in the Bible
THOMAS

JOHN 20:24–28

Thomas undoubtedly wanted to believe, but the story his fellow disciples told surely seemed too far-fetched—too much like wishful thinking—to be true. For reasons the Bible doesn't explain, Thomas had been absent when the risen Jesus first appeared to His disciples. Thomas had to rely on their breathless eyewitness accounts of the encounter.

His companions' story triggered Thomas's investigative instincts. His reply seems harsh, perhaps even a little offensive. But it reflects the deep need of a Five to process something that didn't align with his understanding of the physical world.

"Unless I see the nail marks in His hands and put my finger where the nails were, and put my hand into His side, I will not believe" (JOHN 20:25 NIV).

Thomas needed to be able to confirm, through personal observation and physical proof, what his heart so desperately wanted to believe. It wasn't enough for him that ten of his closest friends testified to having had the same experience. Thomas had to come to belief in Jesus' resurrection in his own way and on his own terms.

The story doesn't end there, of course. A week later, Jesus appeared again to His disciples, this time with Thomas present, and offered the ultimate happy ending for all Fives. Jesus said to Thomas, "Put your finger here; see My hands. Reach out your hand and put it into My side. Stop doubting and believe" (verse 27).

Jesus didn't reject Thomas. He didn't even chastise his doubting disciple. Instead, He offered Himself to scrutiny. He said, in effect, "Do what you need to do in order to satisfy your mind that I am risen."

Jesus embraced Thomas in all of his Five-ness. He removed the barriers to His doubting disciple's faith. In response, Thomas simply cried, "My Lord and my God!" (verse 28).

– Key Scriptures –

WHEN YOU WONDER
HOW THE WORLD WORKS

For ever since the world was created, people have seen the earth and sky. Through everything God made, they can clearly see His invisible qualities—His eternal power and divine nature. So they have no excuse for not knowing God.

ROMANS 1:20 NLT

WHEN YOU GET TOO DEEP INSIDE YOUR HEAD

Therefore we also, since we are surrounded by so great a cloud of witnesses, let us lay aside every weight, and the sin which so easily ensnares us, and let us run with endurance the race that is set before us.

HEBREWS 12:1 NKJV

– Key Scriptures –

WHEN YOU NEED TO DEAL
WITH A RELATIONSHIP

Always be humble and gentle. Patiently put up with each other and love each other. Try your best to let God's Spirit keep your hearts united. Do this by living at peace.

EPHESIANS 4:2-3 CEV

WHEN YOU FEEL LONELY

Even though I walk through the darkest valley, I will fear no evil, for You are with me; Your rod and Your staff, they comfort me.

PSALM 23:4 NIV

WHEN YOU CAN'T FACE YOUR PROBLEMS

We are afflicted in every way, but not crushed; perplexed, but not driven to despair; persecuted, but not forsaken; struck down, but not destroyed.

II CORINTHIANS 4:8-9 ESV

– Key Scriptures –

WHEN YOU'RE SEARCHING FOR ANSWERS

Ask, and it will be given to you. Seek, and you will find. Knock, and the door will be opened to you. For everyone who asks receives, and the one who seeks finds, and to the one who knocks, the door will be opened.

MATTHEW 7:7–8 CSB

WHEN YOU FEEL SEPARATE FROM OTHERS

Let us think of ways to motivate one another to acts of love and good works. And let us not neglect our meeting together, as some people do, but encourage one another, especially now that the day of His return is drawing near.

HEBREWS 10:24–25 NLT

– Key Scriptures –

WHEN OTHERS ACCUSE YOU OF BEING ARGUMENTATIVE

Therefore let us pursue the things which make for peace and the things by which one may edify another.

ROMANS 14:19 NKJV

WHEN YOU NEED TO FOCUS ON YOURSELF

None of us hate our own bodies. We provide for them and take good care of them, just as Christ does for the church, because we are each part of His body.

EPHESIANS 5:29–30 CEV

WHEN YOU FEEL UNPREPARED TO DO GOD'S WILL

If you keep quiet at a time like this, deliverance and relief for the Jews will arise from some other place, but you and your relatives will die. Who knows if perhaps you were made queen for just such a time as this?

ESTHER 4:14 NLT

– Key Scriptures –

WHEN YOU FEEL INCAPABLE

The LORD is with me; I will not be afraid. What can
mere mortals do to me? The LORD is with me;
He is my helper. I look in triumph on my enemies.

PSALM 118:6-7 NIV

WHEN YOU STRUGGLE WITH CYNICISM

Therefore let us not pass judgment on one another
any longer, but rather decide never to put a stum-
bling block or hindrance in the way of a brother.

ROMANS 14:13 ESV

WHEN YOU FEEL THANKFUL

Oh, give thanks to the LORD, for He is good!
For His mercy endures forever. Let the redeemed
of the LORD say so, whom He has redeemed
from the hand of the enemy.

PSALM 107:1-2 NKJV

– Key Scriptures –

WHEN YOU STRUGGLE WITH STINGINESS

The point is this: The person who sows sparingly will also reap sparingly, and the person who sows generously will also reap generously. Each person should do as he has decided in his heart—not reluctantly or out of compulsion, since God loves a cheerful giver. And God is able to make every grace overflow to you, so that in every way, always having everything you need, you may excel in every good work.

II CORINTHIANS 9:6–8 CSB

– Key Scriptures –

WHEN YOU GET CAUGHT UP IN AN IMAGINARY WORLD

God's Spirit has shown you everything. His Spirit finds out everything, even what is deep in the mind of God. You are the only one who knows what is in your own mind, and God's Spirit is the only one who knows what is in God's mind. But God has given us His Spirit. That's why we don't think the same way that the people of this world think. That's also why we can recognize the blessings that God has given us.

I CORINTHIANS 2:10-12 CEV

WHEN YOU NEED ENCOURAGEMENT

Fear the LORD, you His holy people, for those who fear Him lack nothing. The lions may grow weak and hungry, but those who seek the LORD lack no good thing.

PSALM 34:9-10 NIV

– Key Scriptures –

WHEN YOU FEEL INFERIOR

For as many of you as were baptized into Christ have put on Christ. There is neither Jew nor Greek, there is neither slave nor free, there is no male and female, for you are all one in Christ Jesus. And if you are Christ's, then you are Abraham's offspring, heirs according to promise.

GALATIANS 3:27–29 ESV

WHEN YOU DISCOVER SOMETHING NEW

The LORD who made the earth, the LORD who forms it to establish it, the LORD is His name, says this: Call to Me and I will answer you and tell you great and incomprehensible things you do not know.

JEREMIAH 33:2–3 CSB

– Key Scriptures –

WHEN LIFE DOESN'T MAKE SENSE

God is not a man, so He does not lie. He is not human, so He does not change His mind. Has He ever spoken and failed to act? Has He ever promised and not carried it through?

NUMBERS 23:19 NLT

WHEN YOU FACE CONFLICT

A soft answer turns away wrath, but a harsh word stirs up anger. The tongue of the wise uses knowledge rightly, but the mouth of fools pours forth foolishness.

PROVERBS 15:1–2 NKJV

WHEN YOU NEED TO CHALLENGE ACCEPTED WISDOM

If any of you need wisdom, you should ask God, and it will be given to you. God is generous and won't correct you for asking.

JAMES 1:5 CEV

A Prayer for
FIVES

Heavenly Father, when I survey Your handiwork, the enormity of Your creation and intricacy of Your design, I stand in awe. I want to take it in, understand its inner workings, and find the connections that will help me make sense of it all.

Thank You for creating within me a curiosity about the world, as well as the intelligence, logic, and reason to satisfy that curiosity.

Give me the wisdom and humility to know when my quest for knowledge and understanding gets in the way of my well-being and the well-being of others. Help me find the right balance between my need to be alone and my responsibility to nurture healthy and loving relationships. Help me recognize opportunities to use my knowledge and understanding to benefit others and bring glory to You.

In Jesus' name. Amen.

– Type –

6

THE LOYALIST

The Committed, Security-Oriented Type
ENGAGING
RESPONSIBLE
ANXIOUS
SUSPICIOUS

– Overview –

Sixes are reliable and grounded. They have a good sense of "the lay of the land" because they spend a lot of time thinking about their circumstances. They can figure out what's right, and what's potentially wrong, in any given situation. They thrive when they are able to resist fixating on worst-case scenarios.

Sixes place a great deal of confidence in their gut instincts and practical wisdom. Their skills translate well to helping others and improving their communities.

At their best, Sixes find a balance between independence and interdependence. They trust themselves and others. Sixes are capable of inspiring leadership, impactful positive thinking, and meaningful self-expression.

In a work setting, Sixes are skilled at diagnosing problems and suggesting workable solutions. They place a high priority on guarding the safety of a group or project. As they develop trust and rapport with their coworkers, they become more flexible and willing to take chances.

– Strengths –

- Sixes are lovable. They have personalities that appeal to a variety of people. Other people want to be close to Sixes.

- Sixes are hardworking. When they set their minds to a task, they will give their best effort and see it through.

- Sixes are affectionate. They demonstrate their love through their words and actions. They are not shy about expressing their feelings to the people who are meaningful in their lives.

- Sixes are skilled at building cooperation. They can create a team atmosphere, even in a group of very different personalities.

– Strengths –

- Sixes are skilled troubleshooters. They can spot potential problems before they develop.

- Sixes place an importance on trust. They will give their trust to people who earn it. They will also work hard to earn and maintain the trust of others.

- Sixes are committed to their friends and their beliefs. Their loyalty is fierce.

- Sixes respect just rules and authorities, although they may question those rules and authorities to ensure that they are just. Sixes are good citizens.

- Sixes often take courageous stands in order to support the greater good.

– Key Challenges –

- Sixes must learn to embrace their anxiety and make it work for them. They must understand that anxiety is common to everyone. When it's properly processed, anxiety can energize people, make them more productive, and help them focus.

- Sixes must resist the urge to overreact when they feel anxious or stressed. This calls for some self-awareness—understanding what it is that makes them overreact. Once Sixes understand the circumstances that cause anxiety and stress, they can begin to take control of their reactions to those circumstances.

- Sixes must recognize that their fears say more about how they view other people than how other people view them. Many Sixes find that people have a much higher opinion of them than they realize.

– Key Challenges –

- Sixes must guard against engaging in risky behavior as a way of proving to others—and to themselves—that they're not afraid.

- Sixes must pay attention to how other people perceive them. Many Sixes struggle with pessimism and moodiness, which can cast a pall over interpersonal relationships. If Sixes are aware of the impact their "dark side" has on others, they can avoid being their own worst enemies in social settings.

- Sixes must expand their circle of trust. By dropping their guard and giving more people a chance to earn their trust, Sixes will find trustworthy acquaintances in some unexpected places.

– Needs –

- Sixes need their loyalty to be reciprocated. They need to see in others the same reliability and dependability that they pride themselves in giving.

- Sixes need time and space to prepare. In order to minimize the risks and threats they face, Sixes need to process the things that are happening in their world.

- Sixes need to recognize their pattern of replaying their concerns and anxieties over and over again. Once they recognize the pattern, they can find ways to interrupt it.

- Sixes need opportunities to channel their disciplined, practical nature in ways that benefit their communities.

– Needs –

- Sixes need to know that people have their backs. Sixes can maximize their potential when they know they can rely on others, no matter what happens.

- Sixes need to recognize the difference between healthy and unhealthy skepticism. There is wisdom in not trusting people until they've earned your trust. Once they've earned it, though, they should be given the benefit of the doubt.

- Sixes need to resist the temptation to project fears on the people around them as a way to avoid facing their own fears. Instead, Sixes must acknowledge their own individual fears and worries.

- Sixes need to assert their independence occasionally in order to maintain a healthy self-image.

Sixes in the Bible
PETER

The setting is the Last Supper, the Passover meal Jesus shared with His disciples on the night He was arrested. During the meal, Jesus dropped a bombshell on the Twelve: on that very night, one of them would betray Him and the rest would desert Him.

The betrayer stayed silent about his intentions. Ten other disciples muttered to one another in confusion. Only one, Peter, the alpha Six among them, spoke up. His reply may be one of the most Six-ish sentences ever spoken in Scripture: "Even if all the others reject You, I never will!" (MATTHEW 26:33 CEV).

When Jesus informed Peter that he would disown Him three times before the night was over, Peter refused to believe Him. Instead, he doubled down on his Six-ishness. "Even if I have to die with You, I will never say I don't know You" (verse 35).

A few hours later, Peter backed up his words with action. When Jesus' enemies came to arrest Him, Peter drew his sword to protect the Lord. Jesus stopped him and willingly left with His captors.

With his source of support and guidance gone, Peter, in typical Six fashion, lost his self-confidence. He fulfilled Jesus' prediction by disowning the Lord three times. Peter was devastated, though not for long.

In John 21, the risen Jesus appeared to Peter on the shore of the Sea of Galilee. Jesus asked Peter three times if he loved Him. Three times Peter replied that he did. Three times Jesus instructed Peter to feed His sheep.

Jesus restored Peter to ministry after his three denials and gave this Six an assignment worthy of his loyalty. Jesus commissioned Peter to spread the gospel and take care of His followers. According to church history, Peter faithfully fulfilled his responsibilities until his martyrdom. He was loyal to the cause of Christ for the rest of his life.

– Key Scriptures –

WHEN YOU ARE CONFUSED

For God is not a God of confusion but of peace.

I CORINTHIANS 14:33 ESV

WHEN YOU FEEL INSECURE

If you remain in Me and My words remain in you,
ask whatever you want and it will be done for you.
My Father is glorified by this: that you produce
much fruit and prove to be My disciples.

JOHN 15:7-8 CSB

WHEN YOU DON'T KNOW WHO TO TRUST

In God, whose word I praise—in God I trust and am
not afraid. What can mere mortals do to me?

PSALM 56:4 NIV

– Key Scriptures –

WHEN YOU FACE A BIG DECISION

If you seek her as silver, and search for her as for hidden treasures; then you will understand the fear of the LORD, and find the knowledge of God. For the LORD gives wisdom; from His mouth come knowledge and understanding.

PROVERBS 2:4-6 NKJV

WHEN YOU NEED AFFIRMATION

What can we say about all this? If God is on our side, can anyone be against us?

ROMANS 8:31 CEV

– Key Scriptures –

WHEN YOU NEED GUIDANCE

Trust in the LORD with all your heart;
do not depend on your own understanding.
Seek His will in all you do, and He will
show you which path to take.

PROVERBS 3:5-6 NLT

WHEN YOU FIND
YOURSELF PROCRASTINATING

No discipline seems pleasant at the time,
but painful. Later on, however, it produces
a harvest of righteousness and peace
for those who have been trained by it.

HEBREWS 12:11 NIV

– Key Scriptures –

WHEN A CHALLENGE SEEMS TOO BIG FOR YOU

Consider it pure joy, my brothers and sisters, whenever you face trials of many kinds, because you know that the testing of your faith produces perseverance. Let perseverance finish its work so that you may be mature and complete, not lacking anything.

JAMES 1:2-4 NIV

WHEN YOU NEED ENCOURAGEMENT

The one who pursues righteousness and faithful love will find life, righteousness, and honor.

PROVERBS 21:21 CSB

– Key Scriptures –

WHEN YOU FEEL ANXIOUS

In the same way, you who are younger, submit yourselves to your elders. All of you, clothe yourselves with humility toward one another, because, "God opposes the proud but shows favor to the humble." Humble yourselves, therefore, under God's mighty hand, that He may lift you up in due time. Cast all your anxiety on Him because He cares for you.

I PETER 5:5–7 NIV

WHEN YOU'RE TEMPTED TO BE SARCASTIC

Just as damaging as a madman shooting a deadly weapon is someone who lies to a friend and then says, "I was only joking."

PROVERBS 26:18–19 NLT

– Key Scriptures –

WHEN YOU NEED SUPPORT

God is our refuge and strength, a very present help in trouble. Therefore we will not fear though the earth gives way, though the mountains be moved into the heart of the sea, though its waters roar and foam, though the mountains tremble at its swelling.

PSALM 46:1-3 ESV

WHEN YOU FEEL THREATENED

But I consider my life of no value to myself; my purpose is to finish my course and the ministry I received from the Lord Jesus, to testify to the gospel of God's grace.

ACTS 20:24 CSB

– Key Scriptures –

WHEN YOUR SUSPICIONS GET THE BEST OF YOU

I will forgive anyone you forgive. Yes, for your sake and with Christ as my witness, I have forgiven whatever needed to be forgiven. I have done this to keep Satan from getting the better of us. We all know what goes on in his mind.

II CORINTHIANS 2:10–11 CEV

WHEN YOU DOUBT YOURSELF

God is in the midst of her, she shall not be moved; God shall help her, just at the break of dawn.

PSALM 46:5 NKJV

– Key Scriptures –

WHEN YOU BLAME OTHERS FOR YOUR PROBLEMS

Therefore you have no excuse, O man, every one of you who judges. For in passing judgment on another you condemn yourself, because you, the judge, practice the very same things.

ROMANS 2:1 ESV

WHEN YOU FEEL INDECISIVE

The LORD says, "I will guide you along the best pathway for your life. I will advise you and watch over you."

PSALM 32:8 NLT

– Key Scriptures –

WHEN YOU FEAR ABANDONMENT

Though my father and mother forsake me,
the LORD will receive me.

PSALM 27:10 NIV

WHEN YOU GET TOO CAUTIOUS

So be careful how you live. Don't live like fools,
but like those who are wise. Make the most of every
opportunity in these evil days. Don't act thoughtless-
ly, but understand what the Lord wants you to do.

EPHESIANS 5:15–17 NLT

WHEN YOU LOSE CONFIDENCE

For the LORD will be your confidence and
will keep your foot from being caught.

PROVERBS 3:26 ESV

A Prayer for
SIXES

O Lord, I praise You because I am fearfully and wonderfully made. You have equipped me to be a loyal companion to the people in my life. You have given me the opportunity to bring stability and dependability to their lives. You have also given me the ability to recognize potential trouble before others do. I ask that You guide my use of these gifts for the benefit of others and to the glory of Your name.

Father, You know the fear and insecurity that motivate me. You know the anxiety that I struggle with. I ask You to clear my vision so that I may see things as they really are. Give me a sense of Your presence in the midst of my struggles. Give me, too, the wisdom to give my loyalty only to the people and causes that You call me to.

In Jesus' name. Amen.

– Type –

7

THE ENTHUSIAST

The Busy, Variety-Seeking Type

SPONTANEOUS

VERSATILE

ACQUISITIVE

SCATTERED

– Overview –

Sevens live in the moment—and look for ways to fill their next moment. They place a high priority on spontaneity and are drawn to new and exciting experiences. Their constantly shifting attention often results in an impressive versatility. Many Sevens possess a wide array of skills and talents.

Sevens must work hard to rein in their impulsive instincts. Their frequent attention shifts make it difficult for them to "stay in the moment."

At their best, Sevens are able to concentrate their considerable energies and talents on worthwhile pursuits. They find a deep sense of joy and fulfillment. They inspire others with their infectious enthusiasm for life.

In a work setting, Sevens are forward thinkers who bring optimism and a positive spirit to their tasks. They excel at communication. They also place a high priority on keeping their options open and not being tied down to a single location or project.

– Strengths –

- Sevens are adventurous. They will boldly go where others may not. They will take risks physical, emotional, relational in pursuit of their interests.

- Sevens are skilled at identifying potential problems. Their forward-thinking abilities allow them to play out scenarios in their head before they actually occur. It's part of the blessing and curse of constantly looking for something new and better.

- Sevens are encouragers. They love to bring others into their fold and include them in their adventures. They find ways to bring out the best in others.

- Sevens are determined. Though they may appear flighty to some, they place a high priority on reaching their goals.

– Strengths –

- Sevens are energetic. They actively engage with the world. If their energy isn't fully expended in one activity, they will look for other outlets.

- Sevens are unlikely to be dogmatic in their approach to life. They prefer to keep their options open, and they encourage others to do the same.

- Sevens are the life of the party. They embrace everything life has to offer. Their enthusiasm and excitement can be contagious. People enjoy being in the presence of Sevens.

- Sevens give their hearts completely—for a time. Where others may tend to hold back parts of themselves, Sevens are willing to risk hurt and rejection in their relationships.

– Key Challenges –

- Sevens must learn to convert their quick under-standing of other people's feelings into action. In order to do that, though, they must confront difficult emotions instead of searching for a quick "happy fix."

- Sevens must guard against overindulgence. Their pursuit of pleasure makes them prime candidates for gluttony and addiction.

- In their relationships, Sevens must square their own need for freedom with other people's need for stability and reliability. Sevens must realize that their flights of freedom may negatively im-pact the people they care for.

- Sevens must set aside time every day to reflect on their experiences and feelings.

– Key Challenges –

- Sevens must learn to balance their creativity with common sense. They bring a lot of good ideas to the table but struggle to find practical applications for those ideas.

- Sevens must channel their energy into worthwhile goals. They need to recognize the difference between flights of fancy and difference-making opportunities

- Sevens must recognize the difference between the quest for personal fulfillment and self-indulgence. One is a sincere effort to discover God's will and purpose; the other is a waste of time and a relationship destroyer.

- Sevens must learn to listen to allow others to express themselves. In order to do that, Sevens must learn to be quiet.

– Needs –

- Sevens need to be happy. They need to feel pleasure in life. If they don't, they will continue to search until they find it.

- Sevens need to keep themselves occupied. They need to be engaged in things that spark their interest. For that reason, many Sevens prefer to multitask.

- Sevens need freedom. They need to be able to come and go, as necessary, in pursuit of their interests.

- Sevens need to be a part of worthwhile experiences. The fear of missing out on meaningful things is what drives their restless spirits.

– Needs –

- Sevens need to recognize the value of quality over quantity in their relationships. They need to spend time with the people who are meaningful to them and learn to empathize with those people instead of moving on to form other temporary, shallow relationships.

- Sevens need sounding boards when their fears become acute. They need people who will listen to them, encourage them, challenge them, and hold them accountable.

- Sevens need excitement. Since they find excitement in new things, they are constantly on the lookout for whatever is next, whatever is different, whatever they haven't tried yet.

Sevens in the Bible
SOLOMON

As the son of King David, Solomon had the opportunity to indulge his Seven tendencies. Royalty, after all, has its privileges.

First Kings 3 records the events surrounding Solomon's rise to the throne. In this passage, we see a Seven at his absolute best. God made the young king an extraordinary offer: ask for anything you want, and it will be given to you. Solomon surely saw in God's offer the opportunity to satisfy any number of enthusiasms, including fame and wealth.

Yet Solomon was able to focus on a much more worthwhile goal. He asked God to give him the wisdom he would need to lead the people of Israel. God was so pleased by Solomon's request that He gave him the wisdom he sought, as well as the fame and riches he did not.

Solomon exercised his wisdom in some astonishing ways (see I KINGS 3:16–28). As time passed, however, his focus wavered. His less noble Seven instincts got the better of him. He spent thirteen years building a palace and furnishing it with the most magnificent and expensive objects imaginable. He married 700 women, many of them from the royal families of Israel's enemies. In addition, he amassed a harem of 300 concubines.

Solomon pursued an interest in the gods of his foreign wives. He built shrines to the same detestable false deities that God had warned His people about for centuries. This classic Seven began a steep slide from glory that ended with his kingdom being taken from his family line and split into two.

As Solomon reflected on his life, he came to a conclusion that will resonate powerfully with any Seven: "I denied myself nothing my eyes desired; I refused my heart no pleasure. My heart took delight in all my labor, and this was the reward for all my toil. Yet when I surveyed all that my hands had done and what I had toiled to achieve, everything was meaningless, a chasing after the wind; nothing was gained under the sun" (ECCLESIASTES 2:10–11 NIV).

– Key Scriptures –

WHEN YOU EXPERIENCE PAIN

I will bless you with a future filled with hope—a future of success, not of suffering. You will turn back to Me and ask for help, and I will answer your prayers. You will worship Me with all your heart, and I will be with you and accept your worship.

JEREMIAH 29:11-14 CEV

WHEN YOU WONDER WHAT LIFE HOLDS FOR YOU

I cry out to God Most High, to God who will fulfill His purpose for me.

PSALM 57:2 NLT

WHEN YOUR EXPECTATIONS AREN'T MET

Hope deferred makes the heart sick, but a desire fulfilled is a tree of life.

PROVERBS 13:12 ESV

– Key Scriptures –

WHEN YOU GET RESTLESS

Strengthen the feeble hands, steady the knees
that give way; say to those with fearful hearts,
"Be strong, do not fear; your God will come, He will
come with vengeance; with divine retribution
He will come to save you."

ISAIAH 35:3–4 NIV

WHEN YOU ARE EXHAUSTED

Fear not, for I am with you; be not dismayed,
for I am your God. I will strengthen you, yes,
I will help you, I will uphold you with
My righteous right hand.

ISAIAH 41:10 NKJV

– Key Scriptures –

WHEN YOU FEEL GRATEFUL

Hallelujah! Give thanks to the LORD, for He is good;
His faithful love endures forever. Who can declare
the LORD's mighty acts or proclaim all the praise
due Him? How happy are those who uphold justice,
who practice righteousness at all times.

PSALM 106:1–3 CSB

WHEN YOU LOSE FOCUS

Keep looking straight ahead, without turning aside.
Know where you are headed, and you will stay on
solid ground. Don't make a mistake by turning
to the right or the left.

PROVERBS 4:25–27 CEV

– Key Scriptures –

WHEN YOU FEEL ADVENTUROUS

You make known to me the path of life;

in your presence there is fullness of joy;

at your right hand are pleasures forevermore.

PSALM 16:11 ESV

WHEN BOREDOM SETS IN

Be still, and know that I am God; I will be exalted

among the nations, I will be exalted in the earth.

PSALM 46:10 NIV

– Key Scriptures –

WHEN YOU WANT TO TRY SOMETHING NEW

Fear of man will prove to be a snare, but whoever trusts in the LORD is kept safe.

PROVERBS 29:25 NIV

WHEN YOU FEEL TOO FOCUSED ON YOUR OWN GOALS

He makes the whole body fit together perfectly. As each part does its own special work, it helps the other parts grow, so that the whole body is healthy and growing and full of love.

EPHESIANS 4:16 NLT

WHEN YOU NEED YOUR FREEDOM

For you were called to be free, brothers and sisters; only don't use this freedom as an opportunity for the flesh, but serve one another through love.

GALATIANS 5:13 CSB

– Key Scriptures –

WHEN YOU'RE TEMPTED TO BE CRITICAL OF OTHERS

Do not judge others, and you will not be judged.

For you will be treated as you treat others.

The standard you use in judging is the standard

by which you will be judged.

MATTHEW 7:1-2 NLT

WHEN YOU HAVE TROUBLE FOLLOWING THROUGH ON YOUR COMMITMENTS

Commit your way to the LORD;

trust in him, and he will act.

PSALM 37:5 ESV

– Key Scriptures –

WHEN YOU WANT MORE AND MORE

And I am not saying this because I feel neglected, for I have learned to be satisfied with what I have. I know what it is to be in need and what it is to have more than enough. I have learned this secret, so that anywhere, at any time, I am content, whether I am full or hungry, whether I have too much or too little.

PHILIPPIANS 4:11–12 GNT

WHEN YOU GET MOODY

Why am I discouraged? Why is my heart so sad? I will put my hope in God! I will praise Him again— my Savior and my God!

PSALM 42:11 NLT

– Key Scriptures –

WHEN YOU NEED DIRECTION

Your word is a lamp to my feet

and a light to my path.

PSALM 119:105 NKJV

**WHEN YOU FEEL OVERWHELMED
WITH A TASK**

Jesus looked at them and said, "With man this is

impossible, but with God all things are possible."

MATTHEW 19:26 CSB

– Key Scriptures –

WHEN YOU DON'T KNOW WHAT YOU WANT

So don't worry about these things, saying, "What will we eat? What will we drink? What will we wear?" These things dominate the thoughts of unbelievers, but your heavenly Father already knows all your needs. Seek the Kingdom of God above all else, and live righteously, and He will give you everything you need.

MATTHEW 6:31–33 NLT

WHEN YOU GET DISTRACTED

May the words of my mouth and the meditation of my heart be pleasing to you, O LORD, my rock and my redeemer.

PSALM 19:14 NLT

WHEN YOU NEED ENCOURAGEMENT

My power and my strength come from the LORD, and He has saved me. From the tents of God's people come shouts of victory: "The LORD is powerful! With His mighty arm the LORD wins victories! The LORD is powerful!"

PSALM 118:14–16 CEV

A Prayer for
SEVENS

O Lord, thank You for creating in me a unique energy. Thank You for allowing me to experience and appreciate the many good things this world has to offer.

Search my heart so that I may understand what it is I seek in this world. Settle my spirit so that I can learn to embrace the calm of the moment. Keep my eyes fixed on the here and now so that I can learn to be fully present—for my own sake and for the sake of the people in my life.

Channel my restless energy into worthwhile pursuits so that I may bring glory to Your name. Help me understand that only You can satisfy my deepest needs. Only You can give me the completeness I desire. Help me sense Your presence when my impulses threaten to lead me astray.

In Jesus' name. Amen.

– Type –

THE CHALLENGER

The Powerful, Dominating Type

SELF-CONFIDENT

DECISIVE

WILLFUL

CONFRONTATIONAL

– Overview –

Eights feel a strong need to control their environment and the people around them. They have self-confidence in abundant supply and believe that their way is best. Eights are not always driven by ego, however. They desire to use their power to protect others.

Eights will go to great lengths to avoid being controlled by or indebted to other people. In their quest to be self-reliant, Eights will downplay or hide their weaknesses.

At their best, Eights are courageous and self-sacrificing. They are willing to take the heat for decisions that improve the lives of others. At their very best, Eights are heroic and capable of greatness.

In a work setting, Eights are unafraid to step into leadership roles. They bring an energy and intensity to projects that can inspire others. If they are properly managed, Eights can bring out the best in their teams. Their assertiveness can carry a project to completion, usually with some red tape cut along the way.

– Strengths –

- Eights do not lack confidence. Their unshakable belief in themselves inspires others to believe in them as well.

- Eights are assertive. When they settle on a course of action, they will take the necessary steps to make it happen.

- Eights are inspiring. They know how to rally people to their cause or persuade them to pursue a course of action.

- Eights thrive on challenge. They set the bar high for themselves and then work hard to clear it. They also encourage others to challenge themselves and push to do more than they thought possible.

– Strengths –

- Eights are energetic. They are able to draw on enormous reserves of strength and endurance to accomplish the tasks they set for themselves.

- Eights are strong-willed. They are not easily intimidated or coerced. They are not swayed by other people's opinions.

- Eights are comfortable in leadership positions. They embrace the challenge of being in charge of other people. They are willing to take the heat for their decisions—and willing to accept the consequences, good or bad.

- Eights have a passion for life. They possess a can-do attitude that allows them to see the potential for success in even the most overwhelming situations.

– Key Challenges –

- Eights must learn to practice self-restraint. Eights have the opportunity to inspire and motivate others if they resist the urge to wield their power in unhealthy ways.

- Eights must learn to yield to others when it's productive to do so. Eights must recognize that allowing others to have their way in certain situations does not diminish their own power or authority.

- Eights must maintain a clear perspective on their interpersonal relationships. They need to recognize that people aren't necessarily aligned against them but may, in fact, be allies.

- Eights must recognize that self-reliance is an illusion. Everyone depends on other people. When Eights acknowledge and embrace that fact, they can build genuinely healthy relationships.

– Key Challenges –

- Eights must acknowledge the limits of power. Bending other people to your will is not the same as earning their love, respect, admiration, and loyalty.

- Eights must embrace the godly responsibilities that come with power. They must understand the importance of sacrificing their own desires for the greater good and for the well-being of the people under their charge.

- Eights must resist the urge to surround themselves with "yes people" and sycophants. Eights need people in their lives who aren't afraid to question or challenge them, when necessary.

– Needs –

- Eights need to protect themselves from being hurt emotionally. They can withstand physical harm without complaining, but their emotional health is much more vulnerable.

- Eights need to recognize the importance of certain rules and regulations. This helps them resist the temptation to cut corners in pursuit of their own agendas.

- Eights need to harness their "Eight-ness" in productive ways. They need opportunities to lead others in working toward a common good. They need goals that are worthy of their gifts.

- Eights need to balance their self-assertiveness with vulnerability. They need to temper their confidence with a spirit of humility. They need to allow God to mold them into the kind of leaders He can use to accomplish amazing things.

– Needs –

- Eights need people to tell them when they are being intimidating or overbearing. Being aware of how others perceive them allows them to make necessary changes to their leadership style.

- Eights need fairness and justice in their dealings with other people. If Eights sense that they are being treated unfairly, it triggers feelings of weakness and vulnerability, which can cause them to overreact to the situation.

- Eights need to curb their excessive appetites as part of a broader effort to maintain their physical health. They must recognize that their power is not diminished by acknowledging the possibility of personal infirmities.

Eights in the Bible
SAMSON

Samson was destined for Eight-ness. Before Samson was born, an angel of the Lord gave his parents specific rules to follow in raising their boy. Samson was groomed from the womb to deliver the Israelites from the hands of their enemies, the Philistines.

Samson's sense of destiny—not to mention the supernatural strength he'd been given to fulfill that destiny—was reflected in the way he lived his life. Like many Eights, he was extremely self-confident. That confidence, combined with his physical strength, led to some increasingly reckless behavior.

Samson ignored his responsibilities to his people and pursued his own agenda. He flouted Israel's cultural rules against mingling with the Philistines. He bullied his way through his relationships. When consequences came, he bullied his way through them as well.

Like many Eights, Samson sought vengeance when he was wronged. He lost a wager after being outmaneuvered by the Philistines. In response, he went on a killing spree to pay his debt. He left untold destruction in his wake.

Also like many Eights, Samson struggled with lust. His weakness for women—particularly a woman named Delilah—eventually led to his downfall.

His self-confidence curdled into cockiness. He carelessly revealed the secret of his strength, trusting himself to handle any repercussions. Big mistake.

The Philistines cut his hair, blinded him, and chained him to a mill. Some time later, during a banquet in the great Philistine temple, Samson's enemies paraded him out for their own amusement. The assembled crowd taunted the former strongman, not realizing that his hair had grown back.

In the last moments of his life, Samson came to grips with his role as a Challenger—and as a protector of others. He positioned himself between two load-bearing pillars and pushed with all his God-restored might. The temple came down, killing him and the Philistines. Samson sacrificed himself to protect his people, which is the highest calling of an Eight.

– Key Scriptures –

WHEN YOU'RE AFRAID
OF BEING CONTROLLED

But you will not leave in haste or go in flight;

for the LORD will go before you, the God of Israel

will be your rear guard.

ISAIAH 52:12 NIV

WHEN YOU NEED A REMINDER
OF YOUR VALUE IN GOD'S EYES

Then God said, "Let Us make human beings in Our

image, to be like Us. They will reign over the fish

in the sea, the birds in the sky, the livestock, all the

wild animals on the earth, and the small animals that

scurry along the ground." So God created human

beings in His own image. In the image of God He cre-

ated them; male and female He created them.

GENESIS 1:26–27 NLT

– Key Scriptures –

WHEN YOU STRUGGLE WITH FEAR

Haven't I commanded you: be strong and courageous? Do not be afraid or discouraged, for the
LORD your God is with you wherever you go.

JOSHUA 1:9 CSB

WHEN YOUR AUTHORITY IS CHALLENGED

As iron sharpens iron, so a man sharpens
the countenance of his friend.

PROVERBS 27:17 NKJV

WHEN YOU'RE TREATED UNFAIRLY

God will bless you, if you don't give up when your
faith is being tested. He will reward you with a glori-
ous life, just as He rewards everyone who loves Him.

JAMES 1:12 CEV

– Key Scriptures –

WHEN SOMEONE DISAGREES WITH YOU

Have nothing to do with foolish, ignorant contro-
versies; you know that they breed quarrels. And the
Lord's servant must not be quarrelsome but kind
to everyone, able to teach, patiently enduring evil,
correcting his opponents with gentleness.

II TIMOTHY 2:23–25 ESV

WHEN YOU'RE AFRAID TO BE VULNERABLE

Trust in Him at all times, you people; pour out your
hearts to Him, for God is our refuge.

PSALM 62:8 NIV

– Key Scriptures –

WHEN YOU'RE STARTING A BIG PROJECT

Suppose one of you wants to build a tower. What is the first thing you will do? Won't you sit down and figure out how much it will cost and if you have enough money to pay for it? Otherwise, you will start building the tower, but not be able to finish. Then everyone who sees what is happening will laugh at you. They will say, "You started building, but could not finish the job."

LUKE 14:28–30 CEV

WHEN YOU EXPERIENCE INJUSTICE

He is the Rock; His deeds are perfect. Everything He does is just and fair. He is a faithful God who does no wrong; how just and upright He is!

DEUTERONOMY 32:4 NLT

– Key Scriptures –

WHEN YOU'RE AFRAID OF BEING HURT BY OTHERS

In God, whose word I praise, in the LORD, whose word I praise, in God I trust; I will not be afraid. What can mere humans do to me?

PSALM 56:10–11 CSB

WHEN THE RULES GET IN YOUR WAY

With my whole heart I seek you; let me not wander from your commandments!

PSALM 119:10 ESV

WHEN YOU FACE A HARD DECISION

Wait for the LORD; be strong and take heart and wait for the LORD.

PSALM 27:14 NIV

– Key Scriptures –

WHEN YOU FEEL THE NEED
TO TAKE CONTROL

The LORD will keep you from all harm—He will watch over your life; the LORD will watch over your coming and going both now and forevermore.

PSALM 121:7-8 NIV

WHEN YOU GET BLAMED

For the eyes of the LORD run to and fro throughout the whole earth, to give strong support to those whose heart is blameless toward him.

II CHRONICLES 16:9 ESV

– Key Scriptures –

WHEN YOU'RE UNSURE WHETHER TO TAKE CHARGE

So do not throw away this confident trust in the Lord. Remember the great reward it brings you! Patient endurance is what you need now, so that you will continue to do God's will. Then you will receive all that He has promised.

HEBREWS 10:35-36 NLT

WHEN YOU FEEL HELPLESS

You alone are God! Only You are a mighty rock. You give me strength and guide me right. You make my feet run as fast as those of a deer, and You help me stand on the mountains.

PSALM 18:31-33 CEV

– Key Scriptures –

WHEN YOU NEED ENCOURAGEMENT

For God has not given us a spirit of fear, but of
power and of love and of a sound mind.

II TIMOTHY 1:7 NKJV

WHEN YOU ARE OVERLY CONFIDENT

The heart of man plans his way, but the LORD
establishes his steps.

PROVERBS 16:9 ESV

– Key Scriptures –

WHEN YOUR CONFIDENCE SLIPS

This is the confidence we have in approaching God:
that if we ask anything according to His will, He hears
us. And if we know that He hears us—whatever we
ask—we know that we have what we asked of Him.

I JOHN 5:14–15 NIV

WHEN YOU OVEREXTEND YOURSELF

Cast your burden on the LORD, and He will sustain
you; He will never allow the righteous to be shaken.

PSALM 55:22 CSB

WHEN YOU'RE FIGHTING FOR THE UNDERDOG

Listen to me, dear brothers and sisters. Hasn't God
chosen the poor in this world to be rich in faith?
Aren't they the ones who will inherit the Kingdom
He promised to those who love Him?

JAMES 2:5 NLT

A Prayer for
EIGHTS

Heavenly Father, help me never lose sight of the fact that I am not self-sufficient. You are in control of all things, including my life.

You have planted within me seeds of leadership. I ask You to nurture those seeds. Surround me with people who confront me when I need to be confronted, challenge me when I need to be challenged, comfort me when I need to be comforted, and encourage me when I need to be encouraged. Remind me often of the limits of my power and influence. Humble my spirit.

I praise You for the models of leadership in Your Word. Give me the wisdom to learn from those models so that I may use the gifts You've given me to lead others in a way that brings glory to You.

In Jesus' name. Amen.

– Type –

THE PEACEMAKER

The Easygoing, Self-Effacing Type
RECEPTIVE
REASSURING
AGREEABLE
COMPLACENT

– Overview –

Nines see harmony as the key to being loved and valued. They are content to blend in with the crowd and go with the flow. They are quick to help others blend in as well. Nines project a welcoming, inclusive, and easygoing spirit.

Nines are supportive, encouraging, and understanding partners and friends. They provide a safe, grounding presence. They hold fast to their values but withhold judgment of people who don't agree with those values. They work hard to maintain a social atmosphere in which everyone can thrive.

At their best, Nines are able to see multiple perspectives, remain calm and adaptable, provide emotional support and assurance to others, resolve conflict, and maintain an open mind.

In a work setting, Nines are often the glue that holds a team together. Their ability to work in harmony with a variety of personality types is essential to any organization.

– Strengths –

- Nines are humble and kind. Their humility and self-deprecating sense of humor draws others to them.

- Nines are emotionally stable. They avoid drama in their relationships. They can be counted on to provide consistent, genuine concern for others.

- Nines are optimistic. They usually see the glass as half-full. They are able to maintain a positive attitude when others give way to negativity.

- Nines are supportive. They encourage other people to fulfill their potential. Nines will also cede the spotlight in order to give other people a chance to shine.

– Strengths –

- Nines are welcoming. They thrive on bringing people together. They empathize with outsiders and work hard to bring them into the fold.

- Nines are conflict resolvers. They are able to find common ground that isn't always apparent to others. Because harmony is so important to them, they will go above and beyond to reconcile people.

- Nines embrace the simple pleasures of life. They find joy and contentment in small things.

- Nines are able to see issues from all sides. They are willing to consider different points of view. That's what make them excellent mediators.

– Key Challenges –

- Nines must resist the urge to go along with the crowd. They must recognize that the more independent they are, the more they have to offer others.

- Nines must find ways to actively engage with the world around them. That requires Nines to see things as they really are, not as Nines wish they were.

- Nines must carefully govern their self-deprecating tendencies. People often take their cues about how to treat us by the way we present ourselves. If Nines send signals that they are less than important or that their opinions can be dismissed, people will treat them accordingly.

– Key Challenges –

* Nines must examine their feelings and impulses, particularly the negative ones, to see how they impact their relationships. Sometimes negative feelings and impulses can get in the way of the peace Nines seek with others.

* Nines must prioritize their own physical and emotional health. Developing the self-discipline to exercise regularly and maintain a healthy lifestyle will benefit Nines in other areas of their lives.

* Nines must recognize when confrontation and anger are appropriate. In many situations, a brief, uncomfortable encounter can prevent a bigger, even more uncomfortable situation later.

– Needs –

- Nines need stability. They strive to maintain a sense of equilibrium with the world around them. They work hard to avoid situations that might throw off the balance in their lives.

- Nines need to maintain harmony in their relationships. They fear separation from others, so they will go to great lengths to keep the peace with family members, friends, coworkers, and acquaintances.

- Nines need acknowledgement. Their willingness to sacrifice their preferences for the sake of group harmony should not be taken for granted. Nines need to know that their opinions matter and that their participation is desired. They need to be consulted on decisions.

– Needs –

- Nines need structure in their daily routine to help them prioritize what needs to be done. Schedules, reminders, and to-do lists work well in helping them focus their attention.

- Nines need an escape from the drama of daily life. They need an outlet from gossip, backbiting, lies, or betrayals that can occur in human interactions. They need drama-free allies who also avoid fireworks in their personal relationships.

- Nines need to be given what they give others: acceptance and space to be themselves.

TYPE 9

Nines in the Bible
JONAH

JONAH 1–4

God commanded his prophet Jonah to warn the people of Nineveh that unless they repented, He would destroy them. God's command caused a seismic shift in Jonah's status quo. He was used to preaching repentance to the Jewish people, not to the hated Ninevites. For a Nine like Jonah, God's new command was a source of disharmony and anxiety.

In typical Nine fashion, Jonah didn't confront the Lord about his assignment. Instead, he allowed his passive-aggressive tendencies to get the better of him. Jonah boarded a ship bound for Joppa, which was not in the direction of Nineveh.

A great storm threatened to capsize the boat. The crew argued about what to do. To restore peace—in nature and aboard the ship—Jonah willingly sacrificed his own well-being. He instructed the ship's

176

crew to throw him overboard. Before he hit the water, a giant fish swallowed him.

Jonah spent three days in the fish's digestive system. Eventually, the fish vomited Jonah back on shore. Jonah went to Nineveh and preached repentance. The Ninevites repented and escaped God's wrath.

Seeing his enemies worship the same God he worshipped should have delighted the Old Testament example of a Nine, but Jonah's prejudices ran deep. In addition, by reaching out to the enemy Ninevites, he had given up the common ground he shared with his fellow Jews.

Jonah gives in to the unhealthy tendencies of Nines and sits down under a shelter outside the city. He shuts down. And that's where the Old Testament narrative of Jonah ends—with the title character so shaken by the disruption to his orderly world that he can barely function. He becomes so obstinate that he can't appreciate the Lord's mercy. Jonah's lack of activity at the end of his story is familiar to many hurting Nines.

– Key Scriptures –

WHEN YOU QUESTION YOUR CALLING

Blessed are the peacemakers,
for they shall be called sons of God.

MATTHEW 5:9 NKJV

WHEN YOU LOSE SOMEONE CLOSE TO YOU

It is better to take refuge in the LORD
than to trust in man.

PSALM 118:8 ESV

– Key Scriptures –

**WHEN YOU FIND YOURSELF
GETTING COMPLACENT**

Set your mind on things that are above,

not on things that are on earth.

COLOSSIANS 3:2 ESV

**WHEN YOU FIND YOURSELF
IN THE ROLE OF MEDIATOR**

And above all these put on love, which binds ev-

erything together in perfect harmony. And let the

peace of Christ rule in your hearts, to which indeed

you were called in one body. And be thankful.

COLOSSIANS 3:14–15 ESV

– Key Scriptures –

WHEN ANXIETY BECOMES A PROBLEM

Do not be anxious about anything, but in every situation, by prayer and petition, with thanksgiving, present your requests to God. And the peace of God, which transcends all understanding, will guard your hearts and your minds in Christ Jesus.

PHILIPPIANS 4:6–7 NIV

WHEN YOU STRUGGLE WITH YOUR IDENTITY

But you are God's chosen and special people. You are a group of royal priests and a holy nation. God has brought you out of darkness into His marvelous light. Now you must tell all the wonderful things that He has done. The Scriptures say, "Once you were nobody. Now you are God's people. At one time no one had pity on you. Now God has treated you with kindness."

I PETER 2:9–10 CEV

– Key Scriptures –

WHEN YOU YEARN FOR CONNECTION WITH GOD

Make me to know your ways, O LORD; teach me
your paths. Lead me in your truth and teach me,
for you are the God of my salvation; for you
I wait all the day long.

PSALM 25:4–5 ESV

WHEN YOUR WORLD FEELS UNSTABLE

He only is my rock and my salvation; He is my
defense; I shall not be greatly moved.

PSALM 62:2 NKJV

– Key Scriptures –

WHEN YOU'RE FEELING CONTENT

The LORD is my strength and my shield; my heart trusts in Him, and I am helped; therefore my heart exults, and with my song I shall thank Him.

PSALM 28:7 NASB

– Key Scriptures –

WHEN YOU FEEL OVERLOOKED

We must keep our eyes on Jesus, who leads us and makes our faith complete. He endured the shame of being nailed to a cross, because He knew that later on He would be glad He did. Now He is seated at the right side of God's throne! So keep your mind on Jesus, who put up with many insults from sinners. Then you won't get discouraged and give up.

HEBREWS 12:2-3 CEV

WHEN YOU FACE A SUDDEN CHANGE

Jesus Christ is the same yesterday
and today and forever.

HEBREWS 13:8 ESV

– Key Scriptures –

WHEN YOU CAN'T FACE YOUR PROBLEMS

For I hold you by your right hand—I, the LORD
your God. And I say to you, "Don't be afraid.
I am here to help you."

ISAIAH 41:13 NLT

WHEN YOU FACE AN UNWANTED SEPARATION

For I am persuaded that neither death nor life, nor
angels nor rulers, nor things present nor things to
come, nor powers, nor height nor depth, nor any
other created thing will be able to separate us from
the love of God that is in Christ Jesus our Lord.

ROMANS 8:38-39 CSB

– Key Scriptures –

WHEN YOU BECOME RESIGNED TO YOUR FATE

Being confident of this, that He who began a

good work in you will carry it on to completion

until the day of Christ Jesus.

PHILIPPIANS 1:6 NIV

WHEN YOU NEED PEACE OF MIND

The God of peace will soon crush Satan under

your feet. The grace of our Lord Jesus Christ

be with you.

ROMANS 16:20 ESV

– Key Scriptures –

WHEN YOU DON'T KNOW WHO TO TRUST

Blessed is the man who trusts in the LORD, whose trust is the LORD. He is like a tree planted by water, that sends out its roots by the stream, and does not fear when heat comes, for its leaves remain green, and is not anxious in the year of drought, for it does not cease to bear fruit.

JEREMIAH 17:7-8 ESV

WHEN CONFLICT ARISES

If your brother sins against you, go tell him his fault, between you and him alone. If he listens to you, you have won your brother. But if he won't listen, take one or two others with you, so that by the testimony of two or three witnesses every fact may be established.

MATTHEW 18:15-16 CSB

WHEN YOU FIND YOURSELF BEING TOO NICE

But examine everything carefully; hold fast to that which is good; abstain from every form of evil.

I THESSALONIANS 5:21-22 NASB

A Prayer for
NINES

God of Peace, You have created me in Your image, and I praise You for that. You have shown me the power of harmony in my life, in my relationships with others, and in the world around me. You have given me a heart for others. You have shown me the power of compromise and the importance of teamwork.

Give me the wisdom to know when I should pursue my own agenda and when I should sacrifice my own preferences for the sake of others. Give me the strength and confidence to confront others when it's necessary. Help me maintain a spirit of love and humility when I do.

Guide me as I work toward peace in my life so that I may bring glory to Your name.

In Jesus' name. Amen.

– Reference Guide –

SCRIPTURE PROMISES FOR ONES

He does not deal with us according to our sins,
nor repay us according to our iniquities. For as high as
the heavens are above the earth, so great is his steadfast love
toward those who fear him. PSALM 103:10–11 ESV

My grace is sufficient for you, for my power is made
perfect in weakness. II CORINTHIANS 12:9 ESV

For we are his workmanship, created in Christ Jesus for
good works, which God prepared beforehand,
that we should walk in them. EPHESIANS 2:10 ESV

SCRIPTURE PROMISES FOR TWOS

So be strong and courageous! Do not be afraid
and do not panic before them. For the LORD your God
will personally go ahead of you. He will neither fail you
nor abandon you. DEUTERONOMY 31:6 NLT

Come to Me, all you who are weary and burdened,
and I will give you rest. MATTHEW 11:28 NIV

See what great love the Father has lavished on us, that we should
be called children of God! And that is what we are! I JOHN 3:1 NIV

SCRIPTURE PROMISES FOR THREES

The LORD is my strength and my song;
He has become my salvation. EXODUS 15:2 CSB

I can do all this through Him who gives
me strength. PHILIPPIANS 4:13 NIV

For our present troubles are small and won't last very long.
Yet they produce for us a glory that vastly outweighs them
and will last forever! II CORINTHIANS 4:17 NLT

SCRIPTURE PROMISES FOR FOURS

Many are the plans in a person's heart, but it is the
LORD's purpose that prevails. PROVERBS 19:21 NIV

Do not fear, for I have redeemed you; I have called you
by your name; you are Mine. ISAIAH 43:1 CSB

Are not five sparrows sold for two pennies? Yet not one
of them is forgotten by God. Indeed, the very hairs of your head
are all numbered. Don't be afraid; you are worth more
than many sparrows. LUKE 12:6–7 NIV

SCRIPTURE PROMISES FOR FIVES

The LORD is with me; I will not be afraid.
What can mere mortals do to me? PSALM 118:6 NIV

Call to Me and I will answer you and tell you great and incomprehensible things you do not know. JEREMIAH 33:3 CSB

Ask, and it will be given to you. Seek, and you will find. Knock, and the door will be opened to you. MATTHEW 7:7 CSB

SCRIPTURE PROMISES FOR SIXES

Trust in the LORD with all your heart; do not depend on your own understanding. Seek His will in all you do, and He will show you which path to take. PROVERBS 3:5-6 NLT

What can we say about all this? If God is on our side, can anyone be against us? ROMANS 8:31 CEV

Cast all your anxiety on Him because He cares for you. I PETER 5:7 NIV

SCRIPTURE PROMISES FOR SEVENS

Fear of man will prove to be a snare, but whoever trusts in the LORD is kept safe. PROVERBS 29:25 NIV

Fear not, for I am with you; be not dismayed, for I am your God. I will strengthen you, yes, I will help you, I will uphold you with My righteous right hand. ISAIAH 41:10 NKJV

Seek the Kingdom of God above all else, and live righteously, and He will give you everything you need. MATTHEW 6:33 NLT